Cycles of Creation

Shannon Amidon

Cover Art by Sabine Amidon

ISBN (Paperback) 979-8-9993864-0-3

First edition, July 2025
Published by Verdant Voices, an imprint of Verdant Publishing

Contents

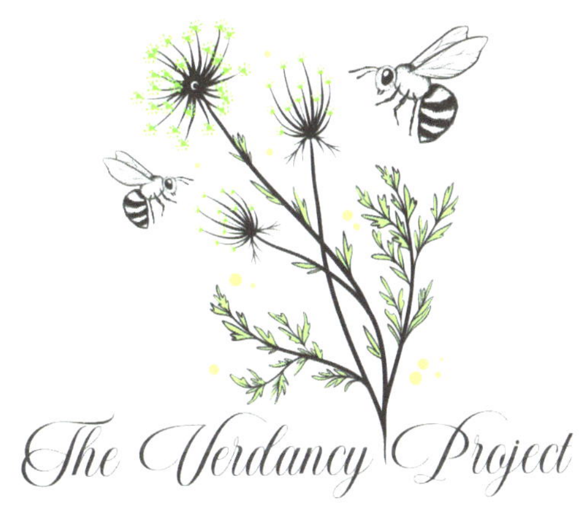

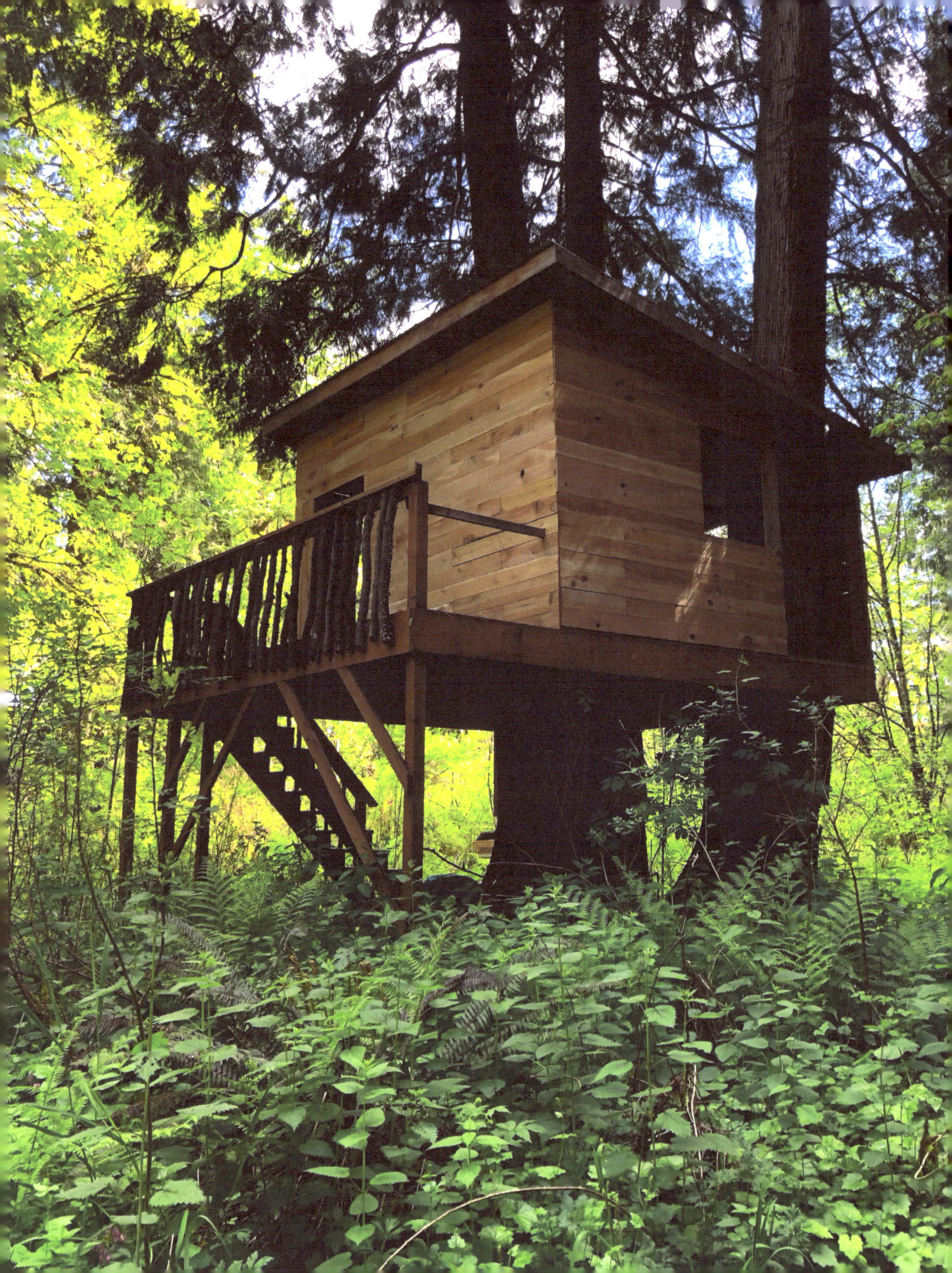

The Verdancy Project is more than a place; it is a living, breathing network of people who believe in the power of art, nature, and shared experience. We are honoured to foster and nourish this ever-growing community, knowing that each connection, each exchange, and each moment of creativity sends ripples far beyond what we can see.

This anthology is a reflection of the first five years—a patchwork of memories, collaborations, ideas, and transformations. It is a testament to the dedication, love, sweat, and dreams that have gone into building something meaningful from the ground up. Within these pages are echoes of laughter, long talks, studio hours, quiet epiphanies, and bold creative risks.

To the artists who have been part of this journey: You have shaped this place with your courage, curiosity, and care. We hope you see yourself reflected in these pages, and that it reminds you of what is possible when art and land meet in reverence.

And to those just discovering The Verdancy Project: May this book serve as an invitation. A glimpse into what is possible when a creative vision is rooted in love for place, trust in process, and commitment to community. We hope it inspires you to dream your own version into being.

The work continues. The land grows, seasons shift, and new artists arrive with stories still unwritten. We carry what we've learned into the next five years and beyond, with open hands, open hearts, and a deep belief in the transformative power of this work.

'A creative life is an amplified life. It's a bigger life, a happier life, an expanded life, and a hell of a lot more interesting life.'
- Elizabeth Gilbert

The Birth of a Dream

As a professional visual artist, I've had the opportunity to participate in a variety of artist residencies around the world. These experiences have been transformative—expanding my creative perspective and strengthening my connection to my work. When my partner and I decided to start a family, I was concerned about how it might affect my creativity and career.

In 2012, I became a mother—an incredible and daunting journey of its own and I was determined not to let go of my identity as an artist. Thankfully, my daily studio rhythm didn't change too drastically. In fact, becoming a parent made me more focused and efficient. Creating is essential to who I am, and I knew I couldn't let that part of myself fade.. I was able to bring my daughter into the studio with me, to openings, exhibitions, open studios, etc. What I didn't anticipate was that opportunities like artist residencies would be almost impossible to participate in. There are a number of reasons for this, mainly time and finances. Most residencies are a minimum of a month long and do not allow you to bring a child or partner.

That is when the seed for The Verdancy Project was planted. I began to research residencies that support or cater to parents. There are a few out there and the number is growing. Often, they are highly competitive and difficult to get into. Some you can bring your child and others they give you a stipend to pay for childcare. I've always believed that if you can't find what you are looking for, you should create it yourself. Don't wait for someone else—or rely on gatekeepers.

I decided to create my own artist residency program for parents. As I started planning, reading, and researching, I soon learned that it's not just parents who experience these challenges participating in residencies; caretakers, working artists, and artists with disabilities all need, want, and deserve to have the opportunity to experience a residency, but have largely been excluded by the typical available residency models.

After years of planning, plotting, and daydreaming, The Verdancy Project (TVP) was officially launched in the Summer of 2020. TVP is a heart-centred, multidisciplinary, community-oriented art initiative with a mission of fostering curiosity and inspiring environmental stewardship. We offer creative residencies, retreats, community art projects, events, and workshops. We do not impose any expectations of productivity on our artists in residence. There are no project or production requirements. We think it's important to normalize rest, idea generation, gestation, and time for artists to just be present without the expectations of output. We understand how important it is to plant the seeds of creativity and to have time to rest, explore, and cultivate ideas.

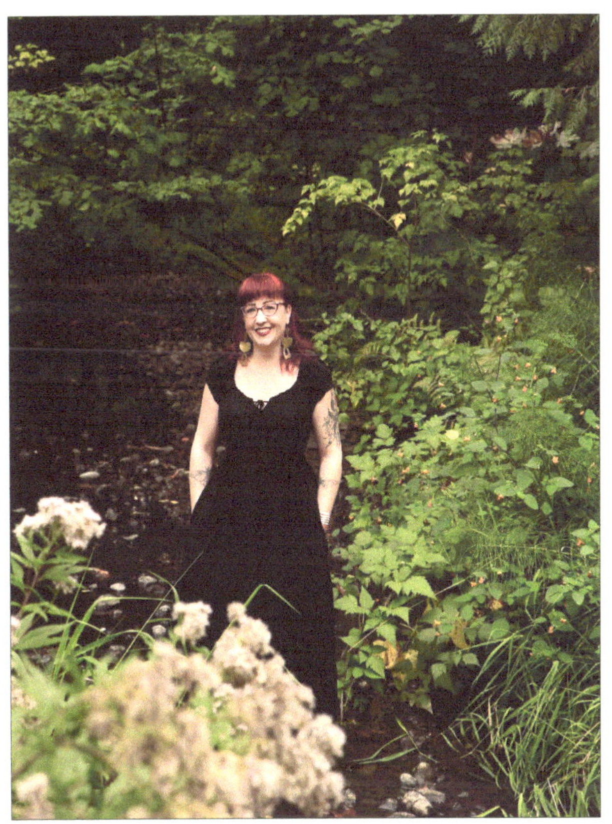

Five years later The Verdancy Project has grown into something I could never have imagined. The artist, community and supporters of TVP have been absolutely incredible. The friendships, projects, collaborations and art made here have been life changing. I am honoured to be able to facilitate this residency, and to share in the experience of this space with so many wonderful people.

Shannon Amidon, Founder and Director

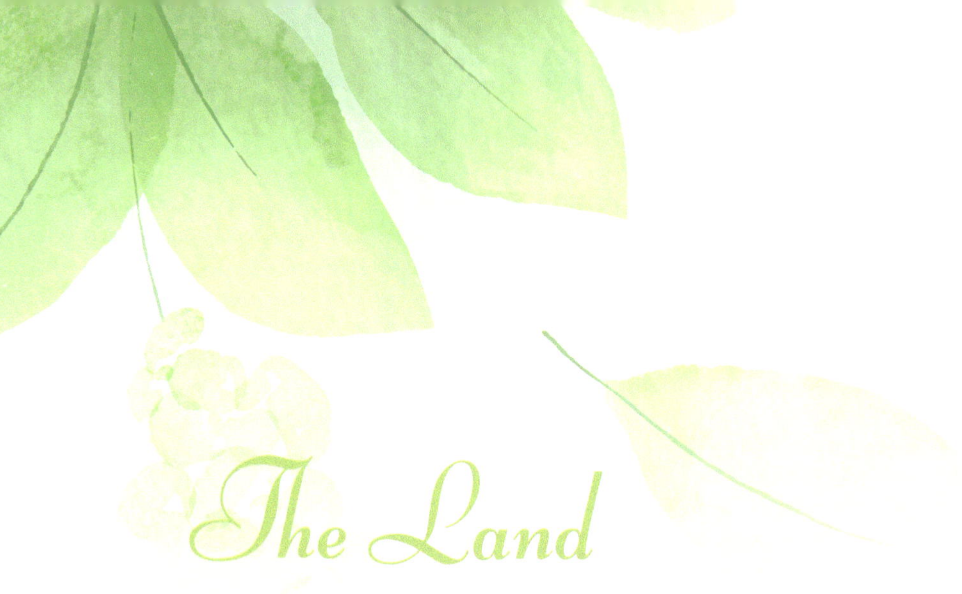

The Land

The land is the heart of The Verdancy Project. It nourishes, holds, collaborates, protects, and inspires. Our name—The Verdancy Project—was born from this lush, ever-changing landscape. This place is not just a backdrop; it is a living, breathing presence. A collaborator in every piece of art, every moment of reflection, every seed of an idea that quietly takes root.

The land teaches us. It reminds us that creativity, like nature, moves in cycles of stillness and bloom, decay and renewal. It asks us to slow down, to pay attention, to listen to birdsong, wind and water. It invites us to touch moss, go off-trail and get dirt under our fingernails. The land encourages rest as much as productivity, noticing as much as making.

Situated on four-and-a-half acres in Troutdale, Oregon, this place is a patchwork of wild and tended spaces. Our dye garden is filled with color and intention. The pollinator habitat is alive with bees and butterflies. There's a treehouse nestled high in the cedars, a woven willow den hidden like a secret, a little caravan inviting quiet nights and star-filled dreams. Artists read and dream in the book shed and nature library, gather by the key tree, and rest near the flowing creek that cuts gently through the land. Blueberries and blackberries ripen in the sun. The bee tree hums with quiet purpose.

Every inch of this land holds memory. It holds the laughter of past gatherings, the footsteps of artists walking in meditation, the silence of someone finding their way back to themselves. I have cried here, dreamed here, and rediscovered my own creative fire more times than I can count.

This place has shaped me. It has taught me how to hold space, how to listen, how to be in right relationship, not just with the earth, but with the people who come here seeking something they may not yet have words for. It is an anchor and a mirror, reminding us of our connection to something older, wilder, and deeply wise.

The land is our partner, our teacher, our sanctuary. Everything we do at The Verdancy Project begins here.

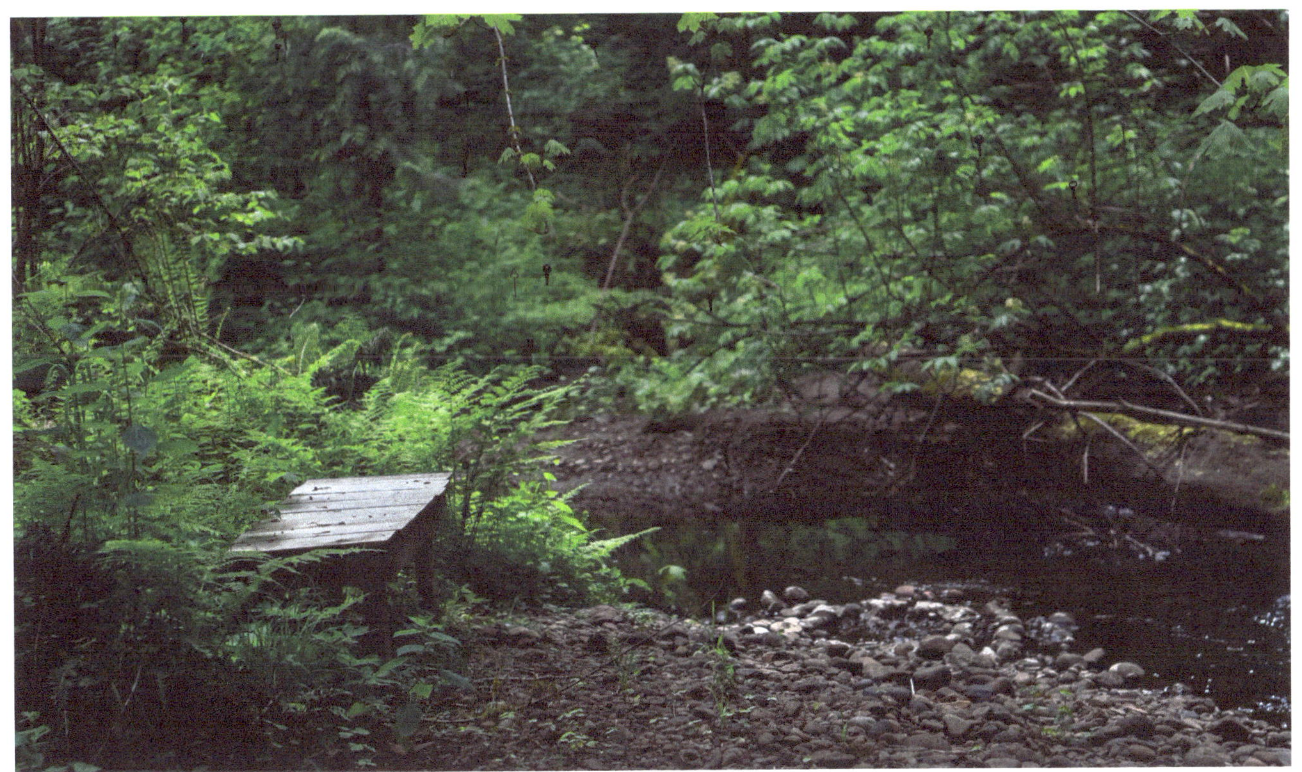

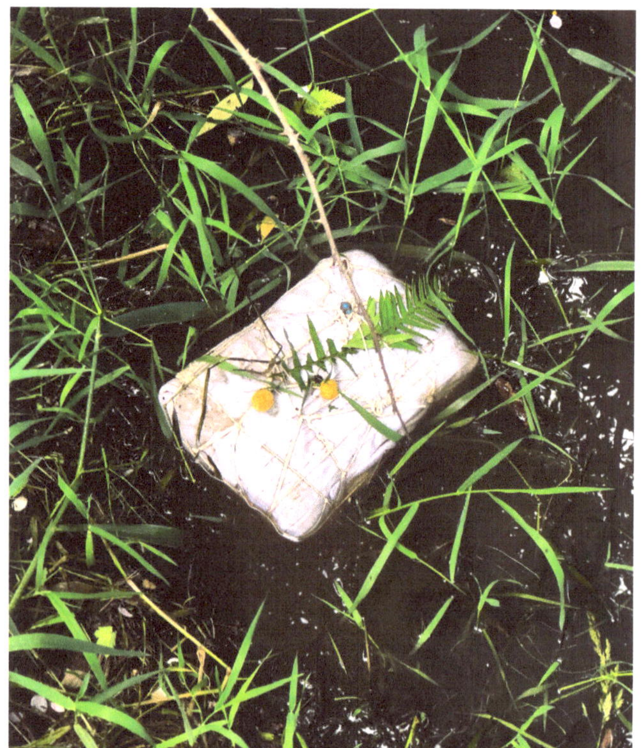

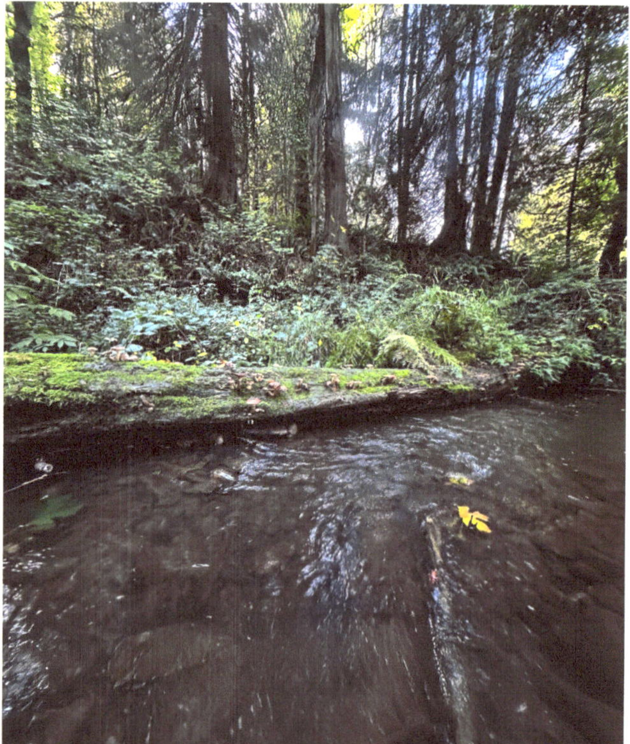

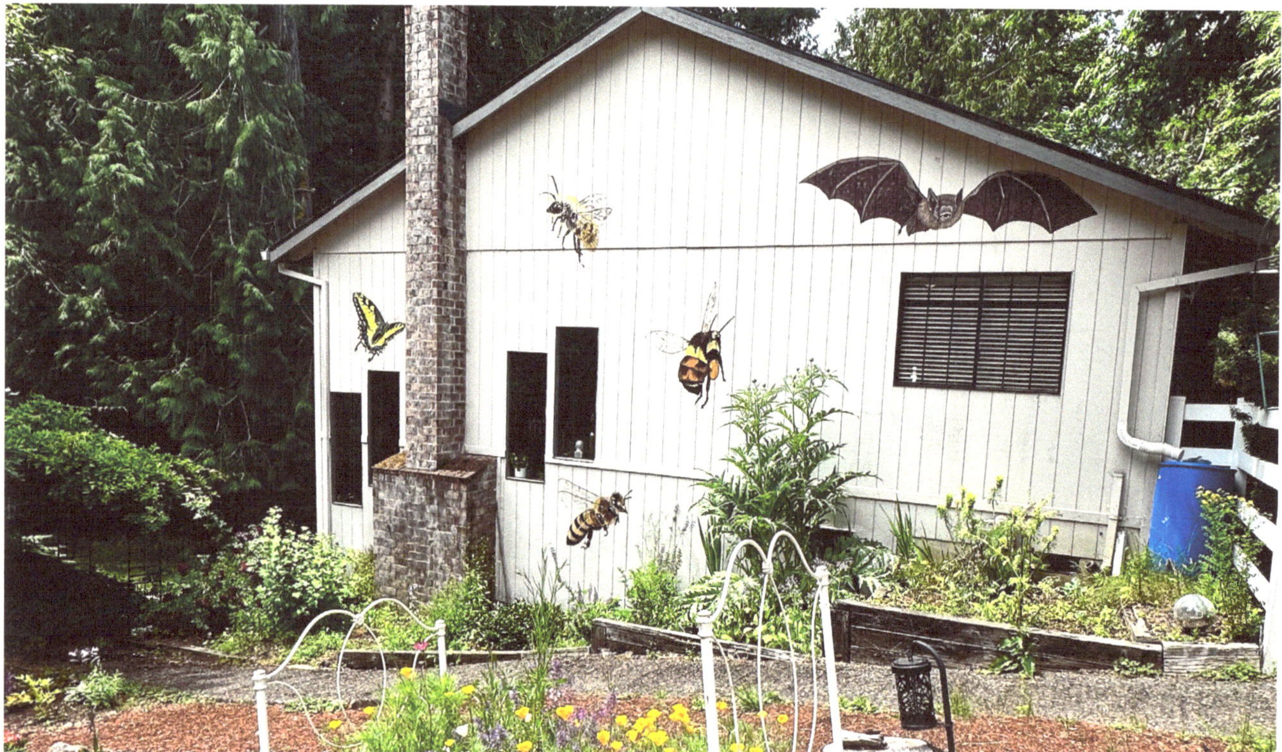

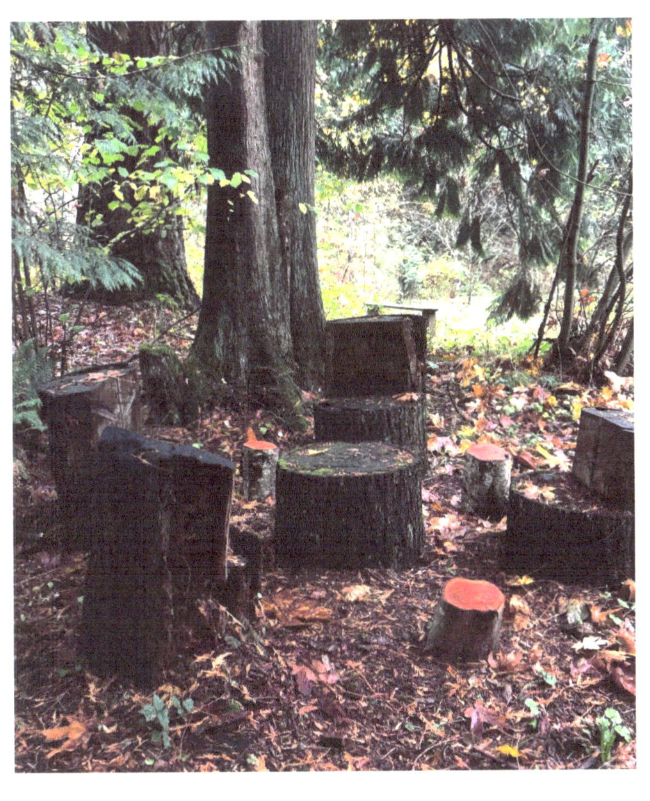

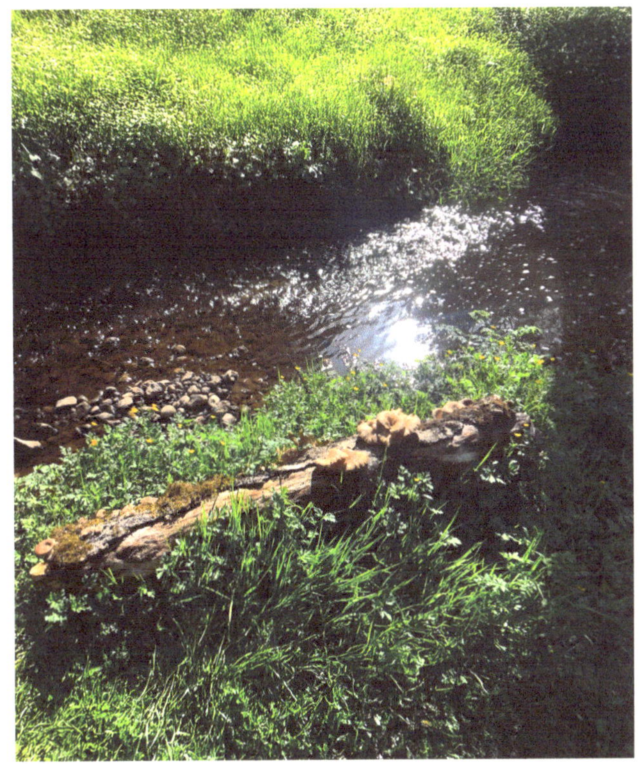

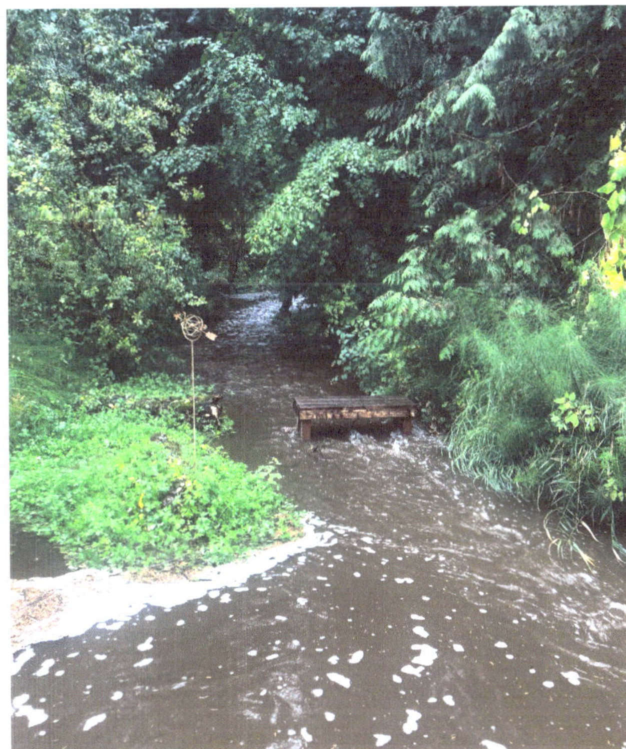

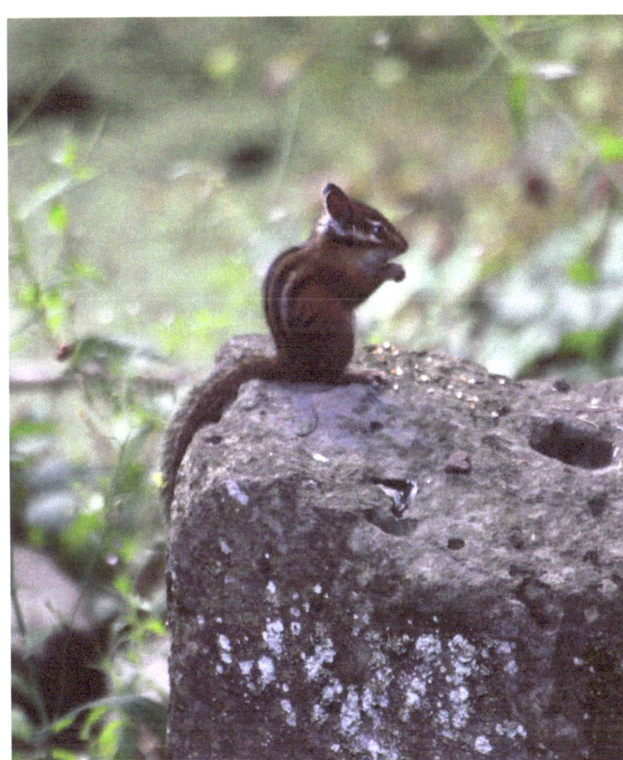

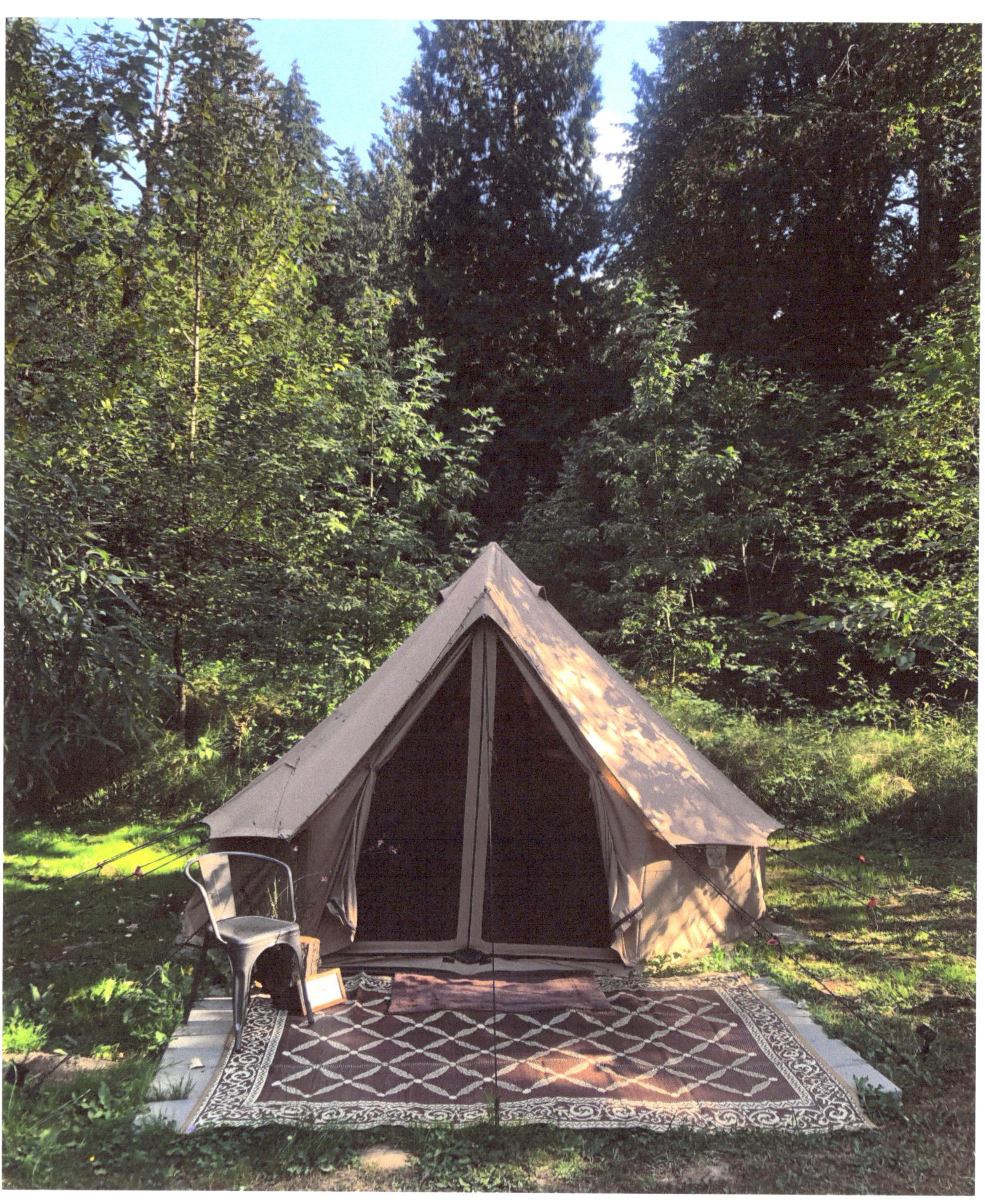

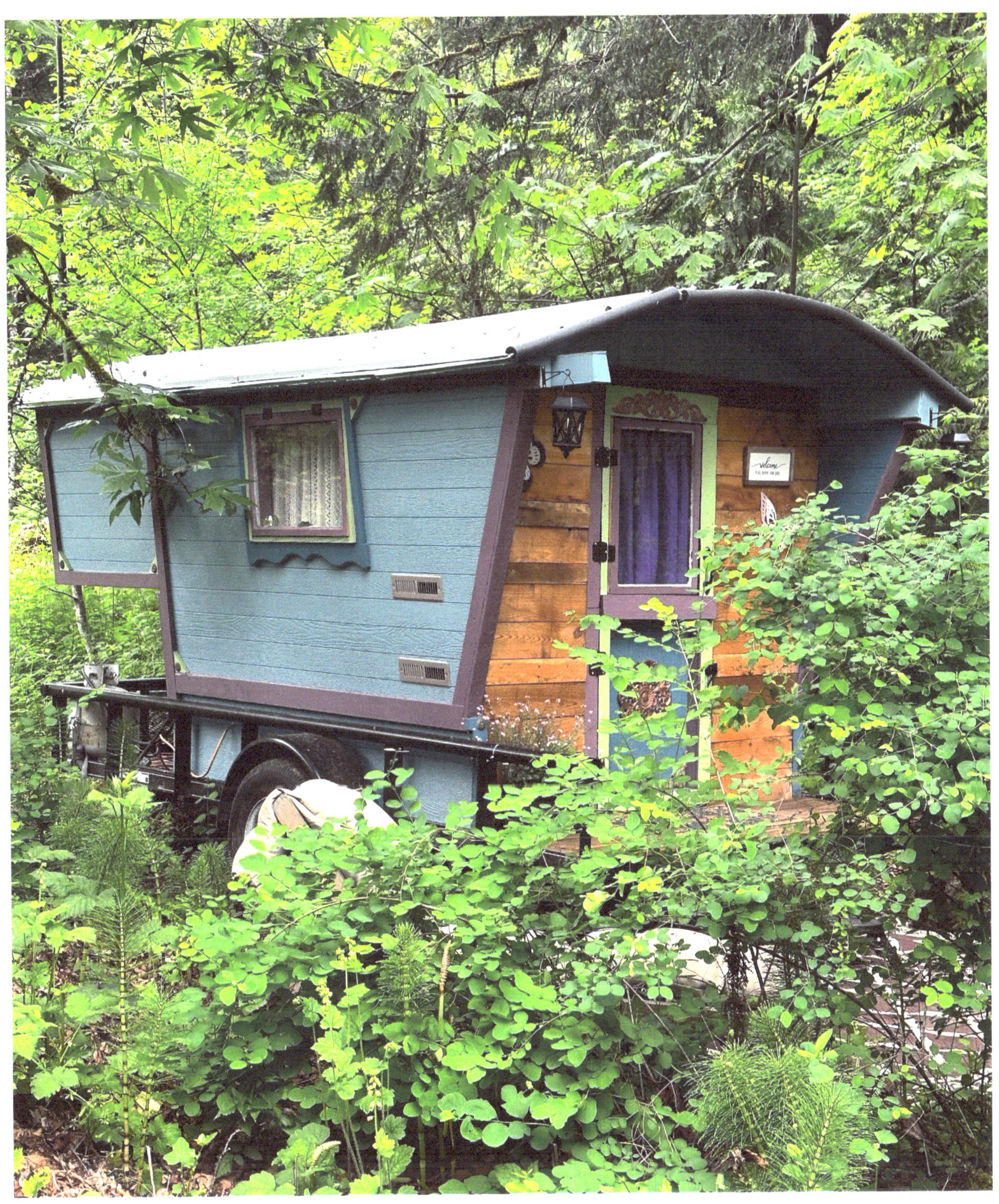
Welcome

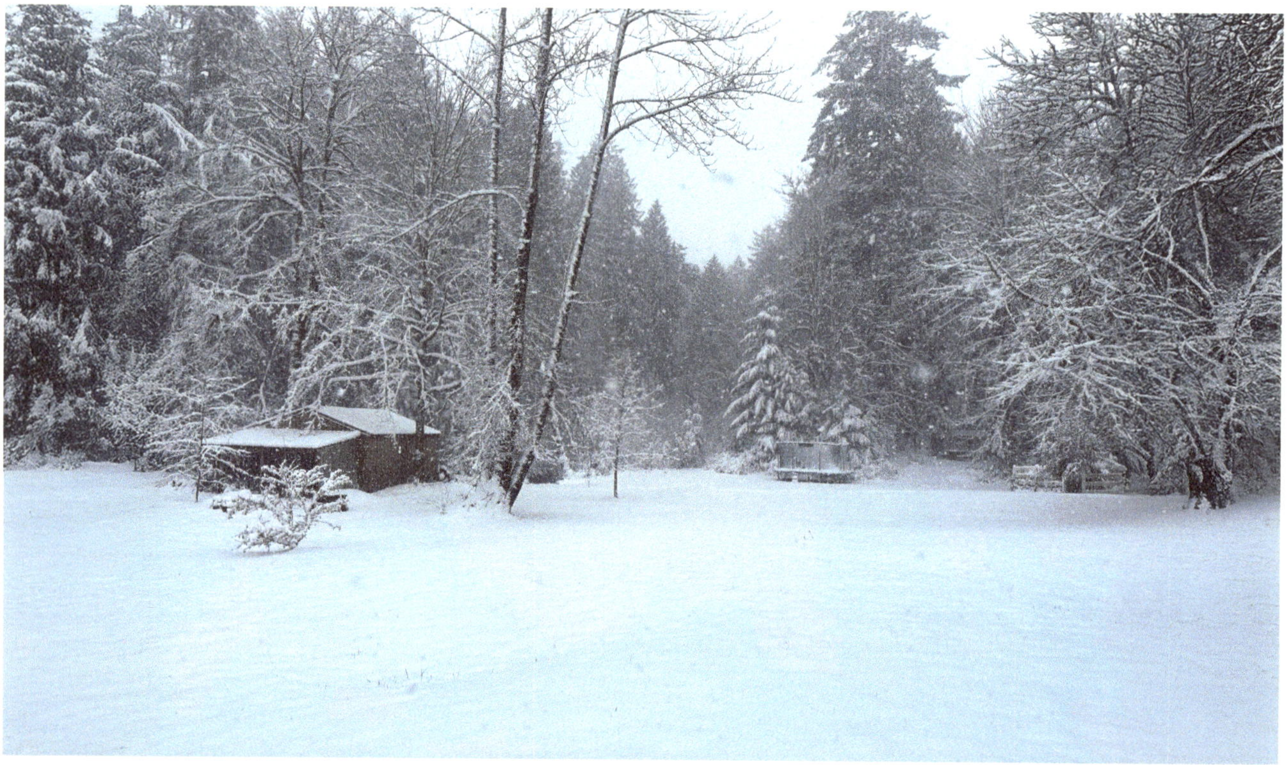

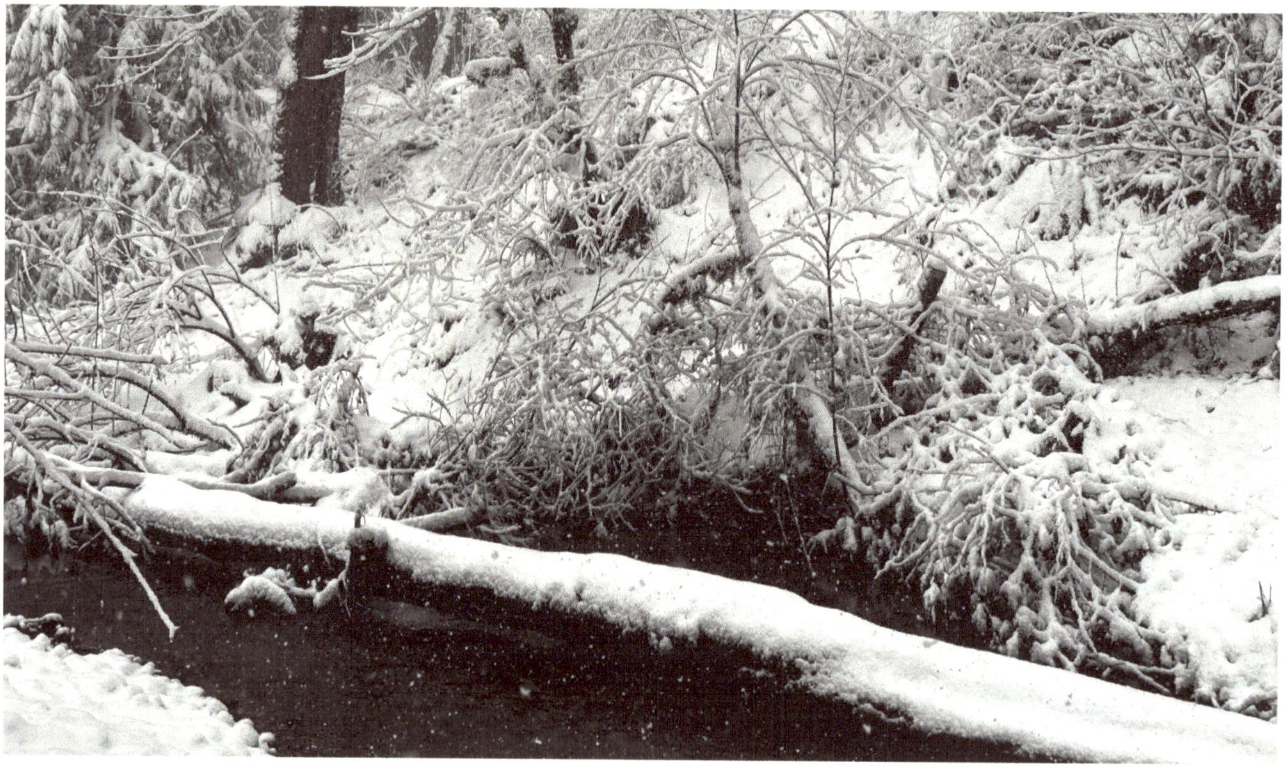

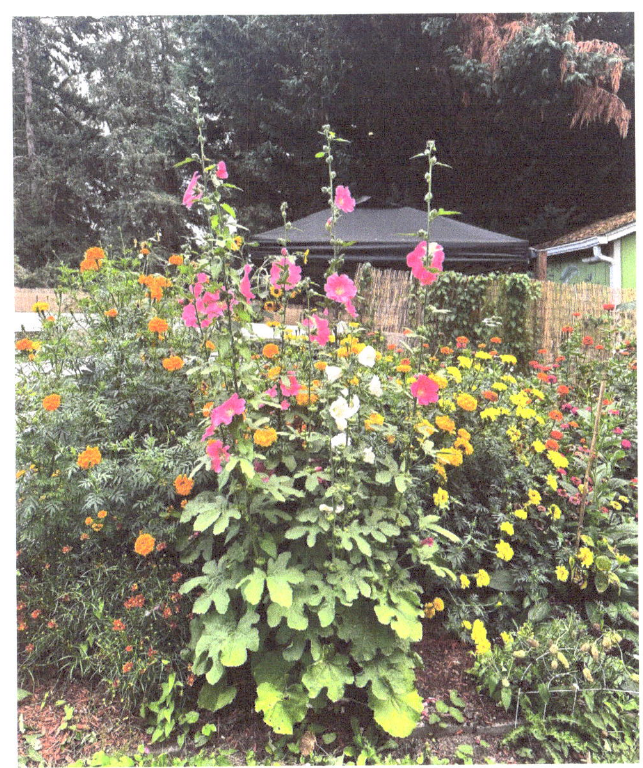

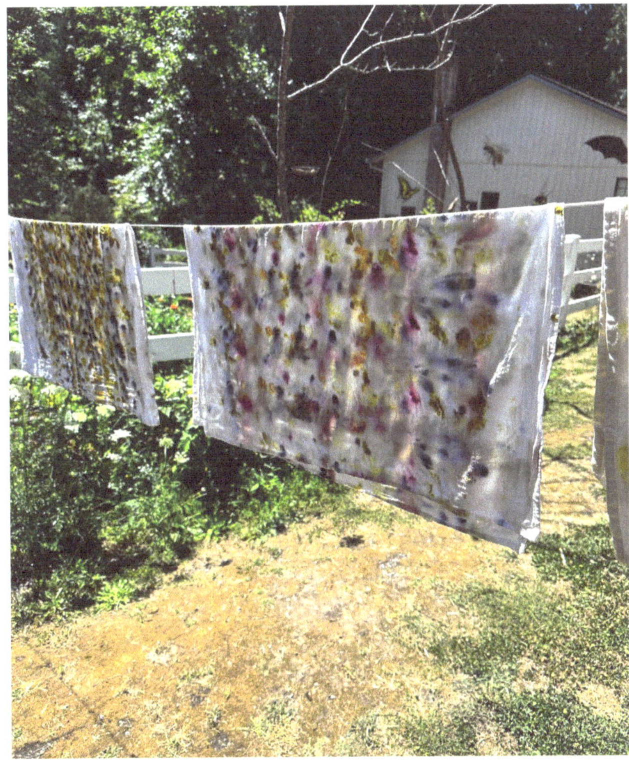

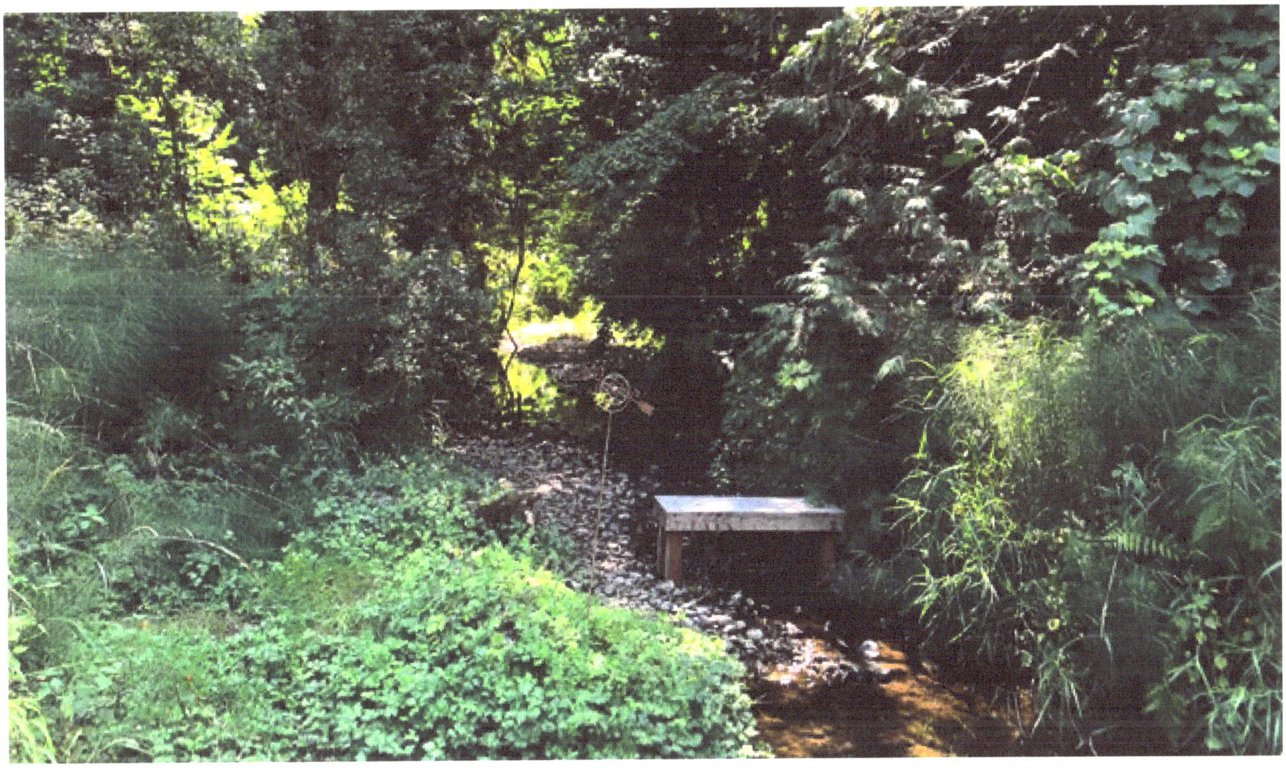

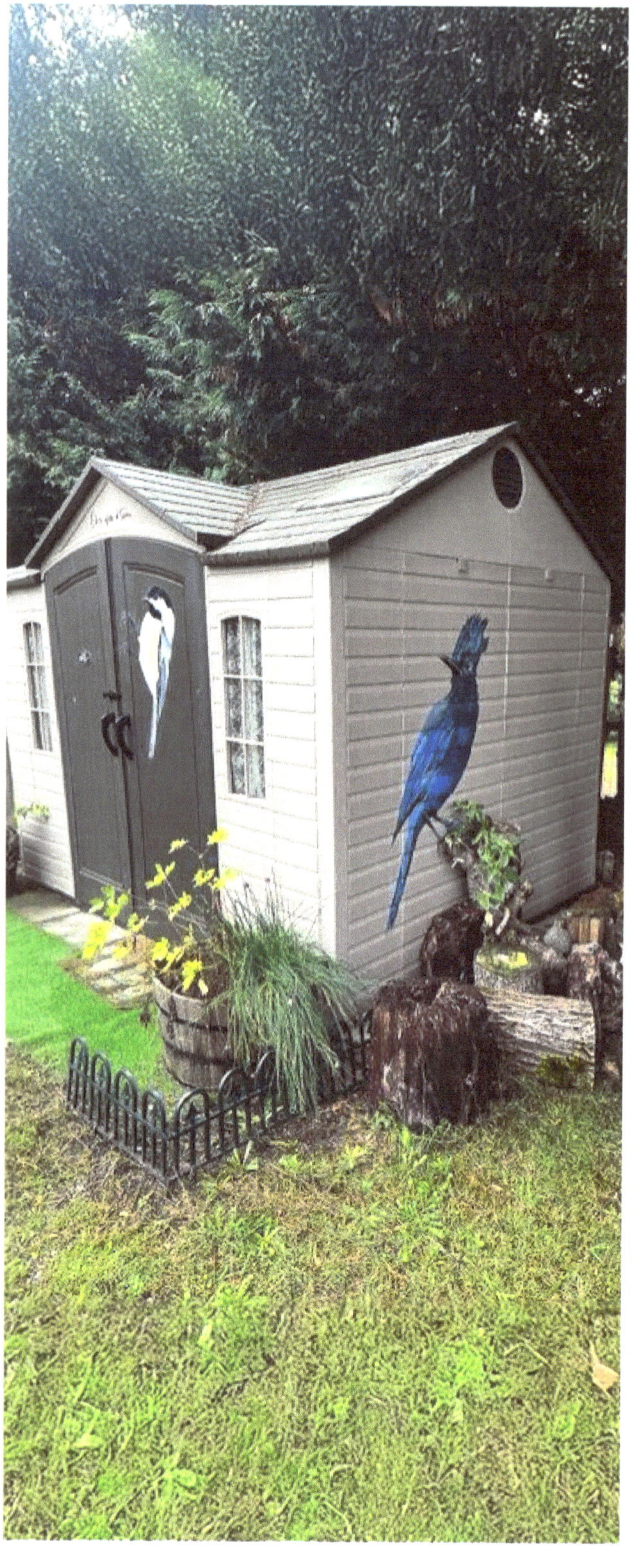

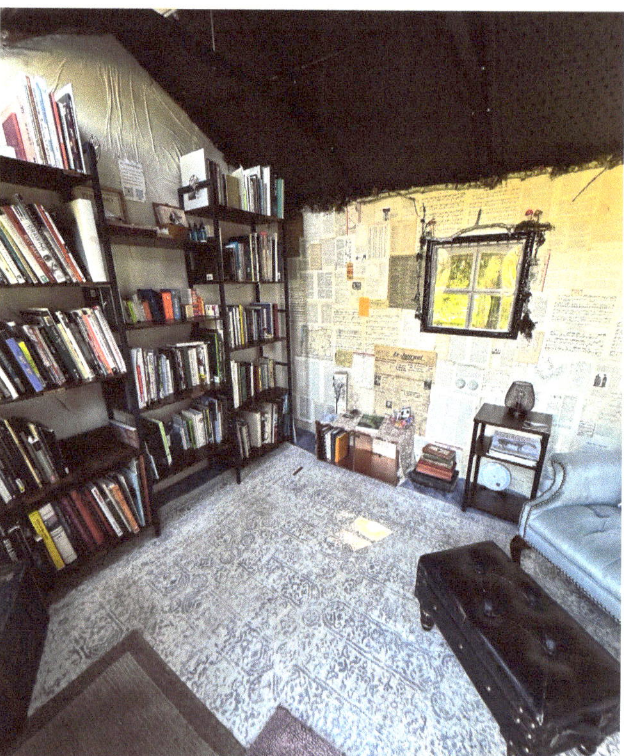

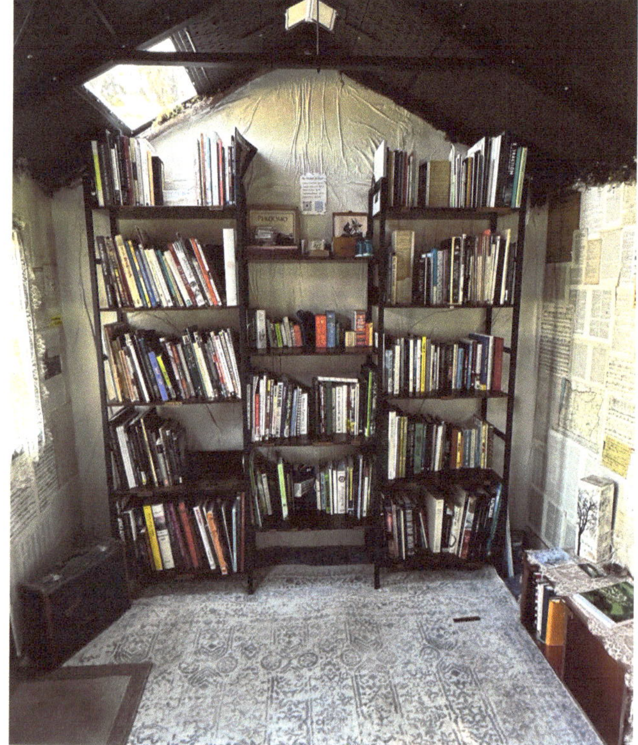

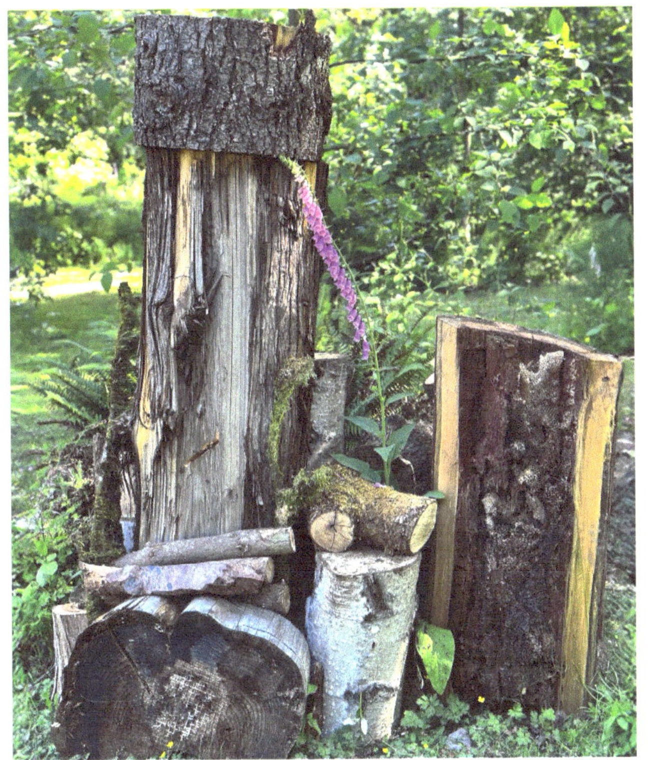

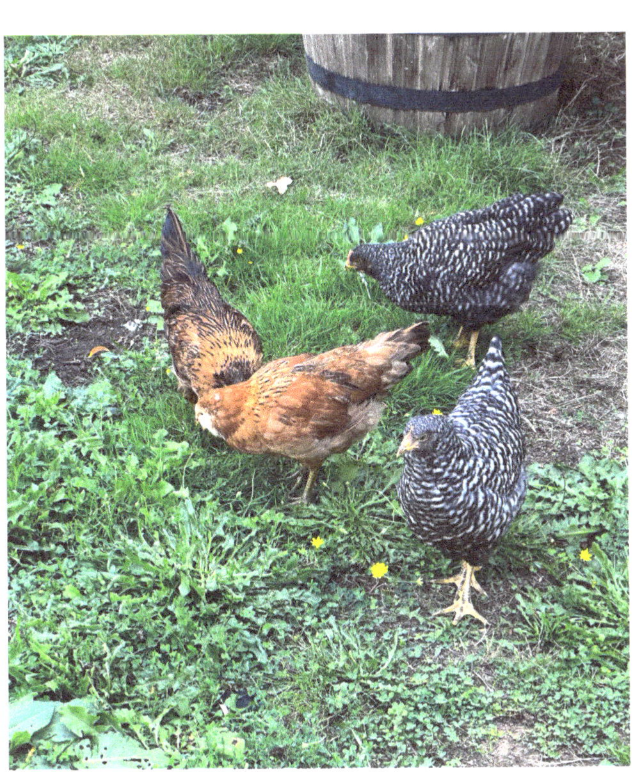

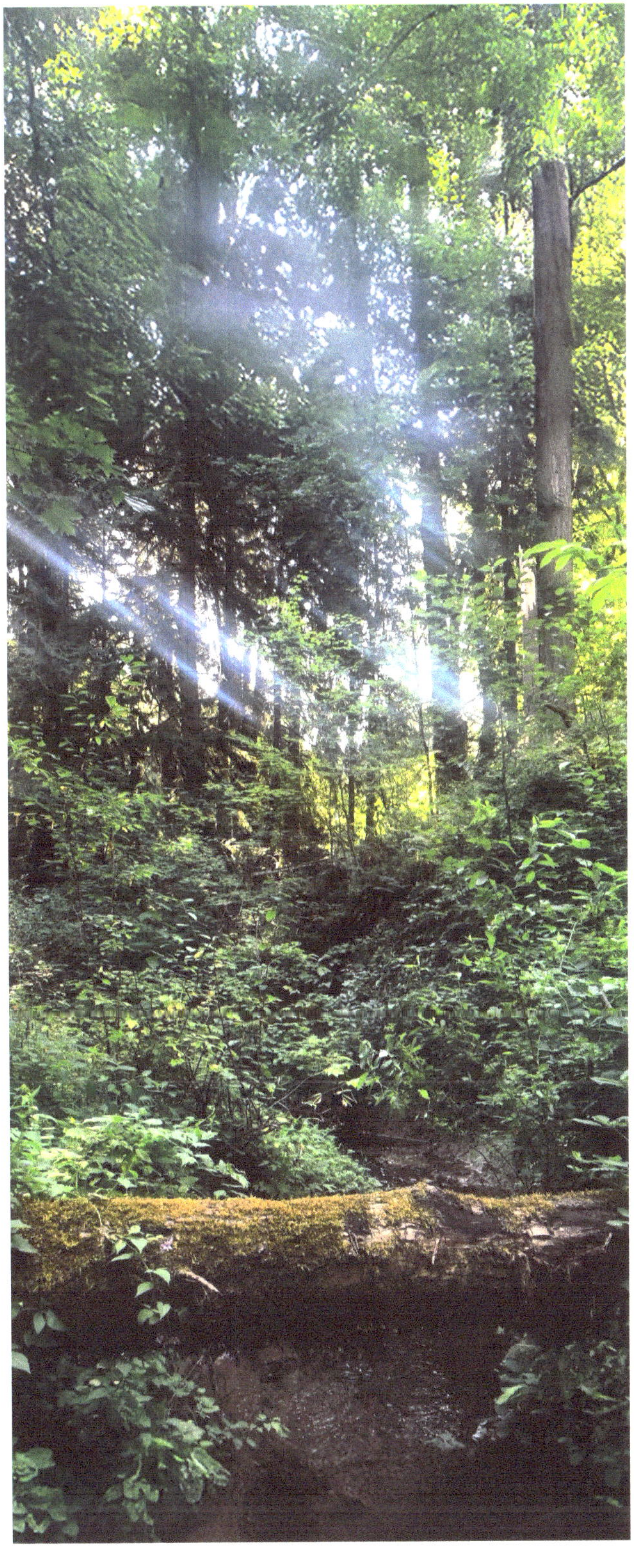

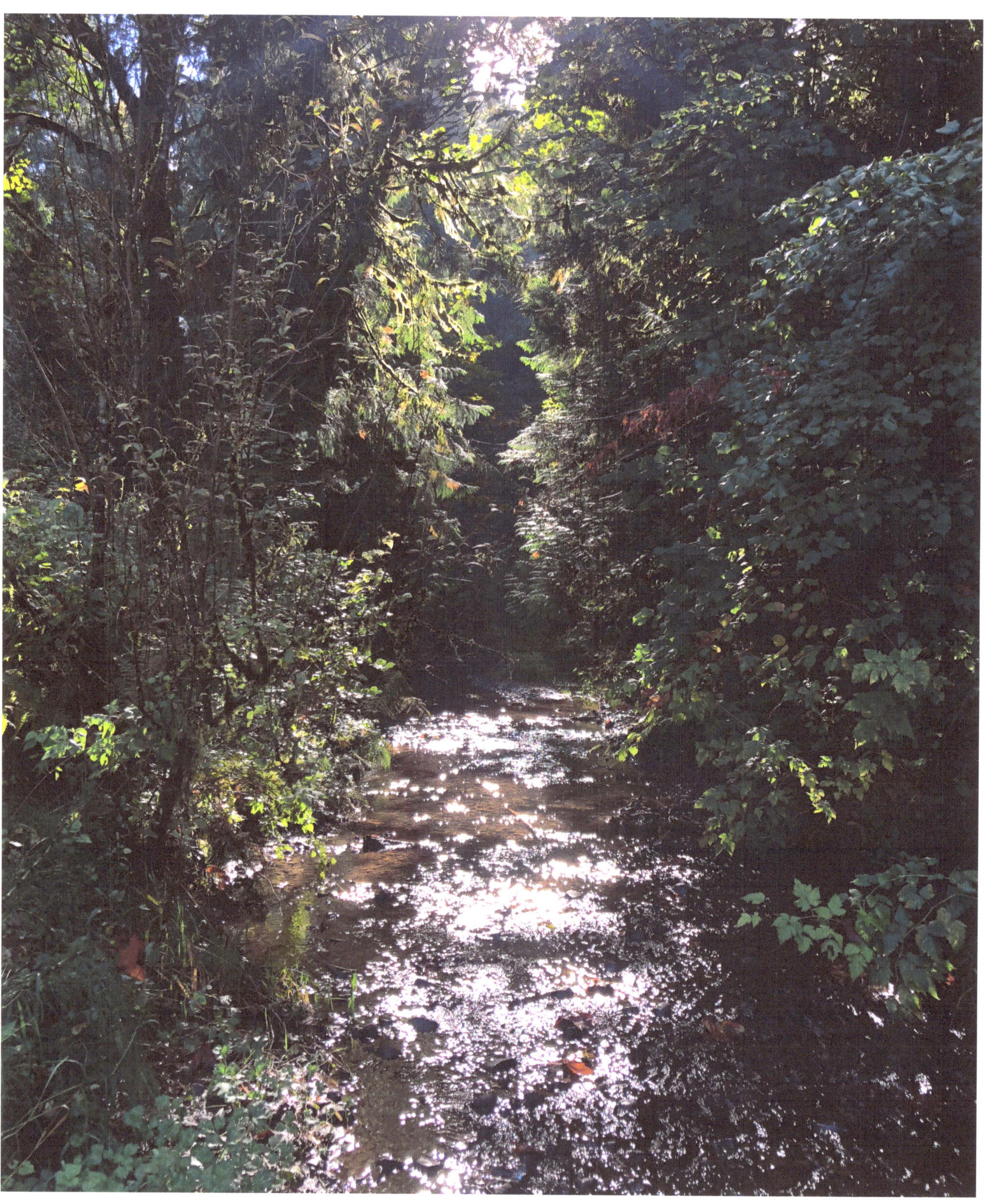

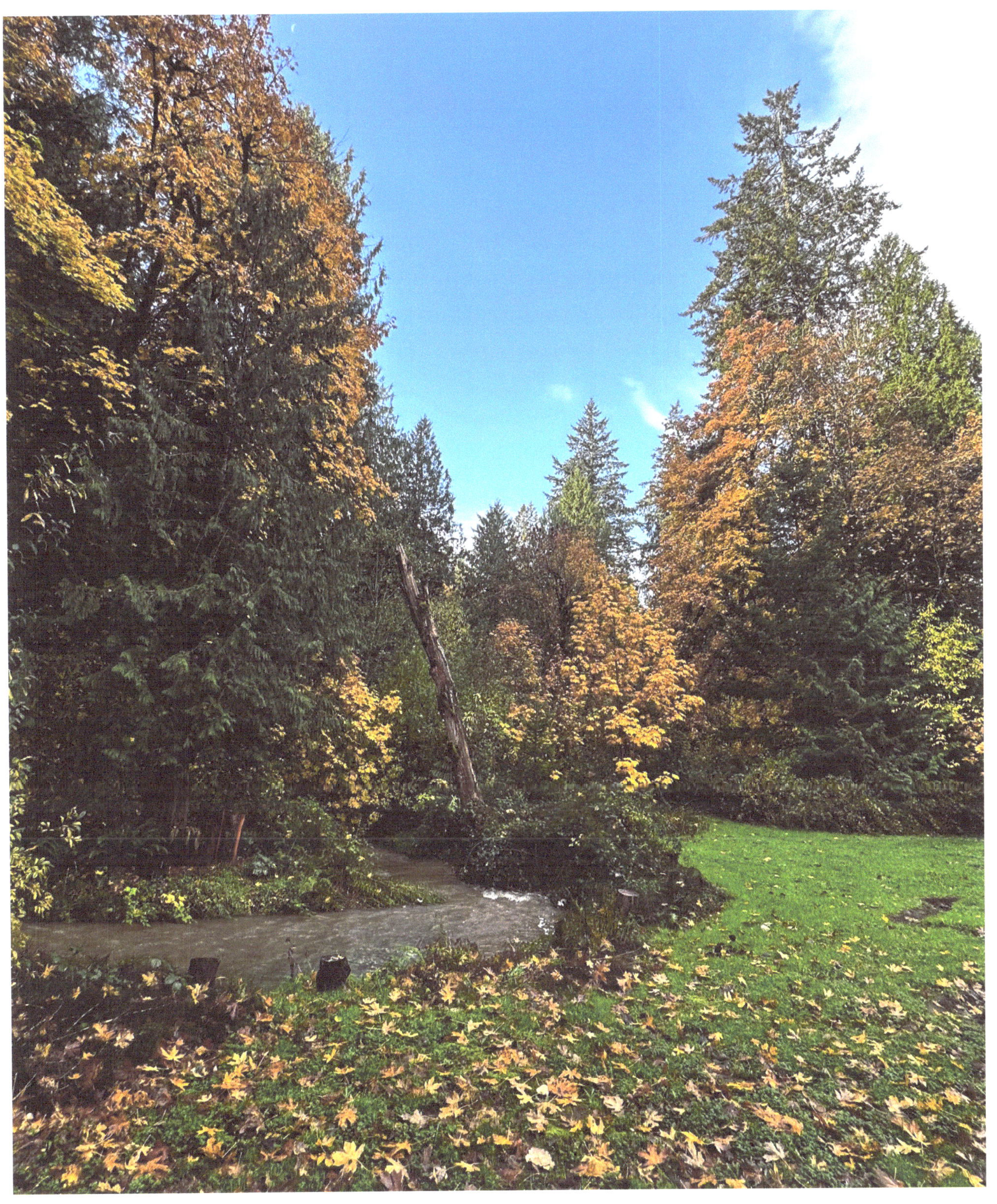

Our Community

Community is the soul of The Verdancy Project. Our mission extends beyond the artists we host, reaching into the wider world through workshops, events, and collaborative projects. We believe in creating spaces where creativity and nature intersect, where knowledge is shared, and where meaningful connections take root and flourish.

Through our **nature-based workshops**, we invite people to slow down, observe, and engage with the world around them in new ways. From natural pigment making and nature journaling to cyanotypes, color theory, lumen printing, and the intersection of art and science, each gathering is an opportunity to explore, learn, and create alongside the land.

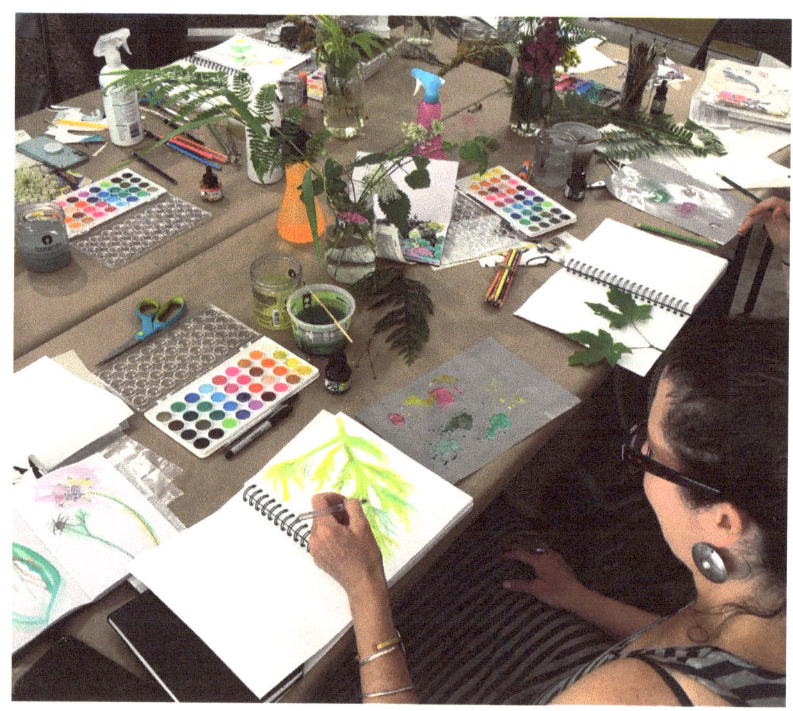

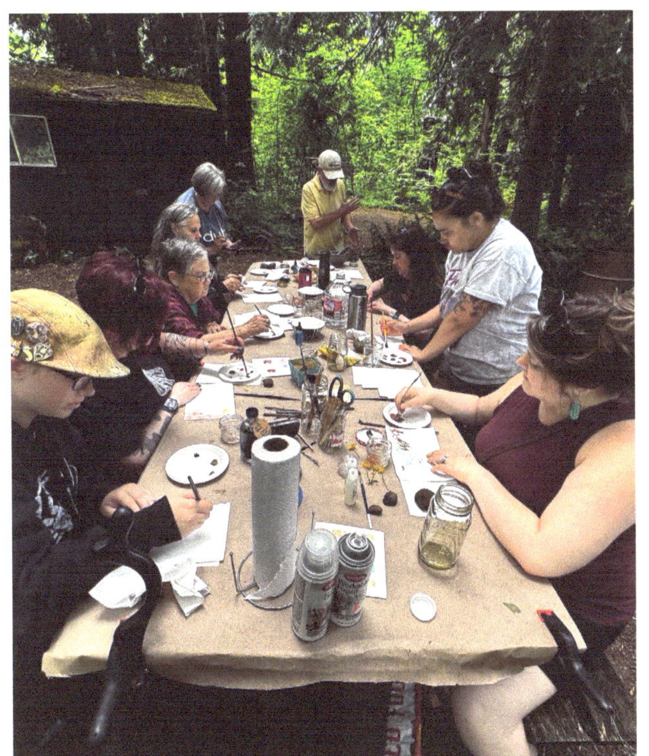

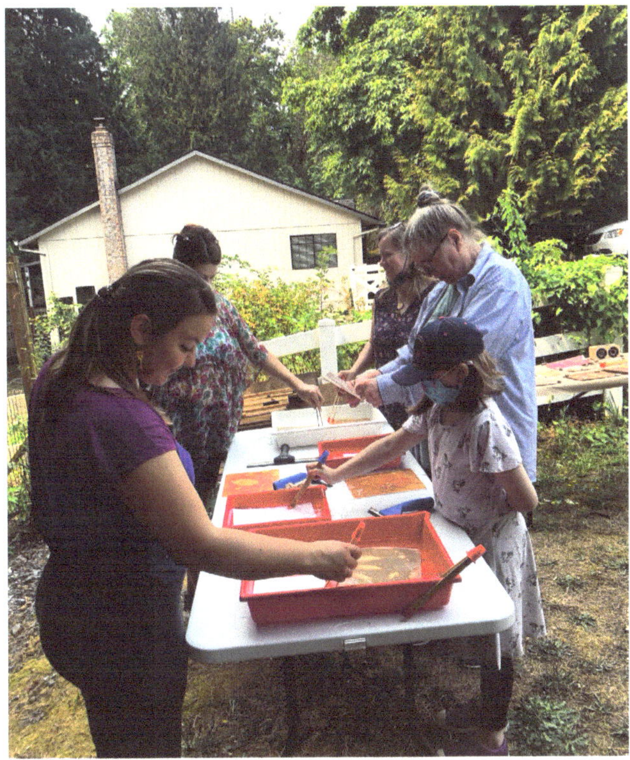

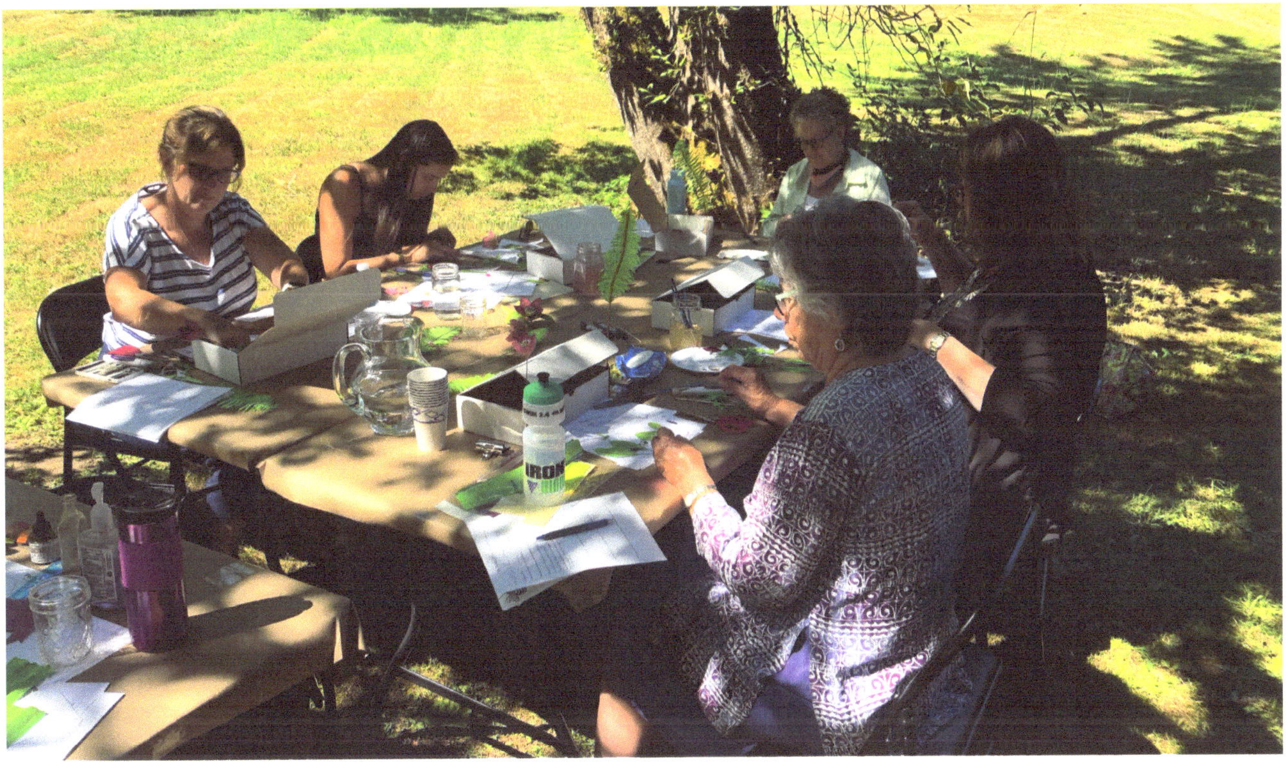

One of our most cherished events, the **Art & Seed Swap**, has brought together over one hundred twentyfive artists and community members to create original seed packet artwork and exchange seeds, an act as symbolic as it is practical. Seed sharing is an ancient practice, a quiet yet powerful act of resilience. In a time of rapid environmental change, preserving the biodiversity of our crops is an essential gesture of hope for the future.

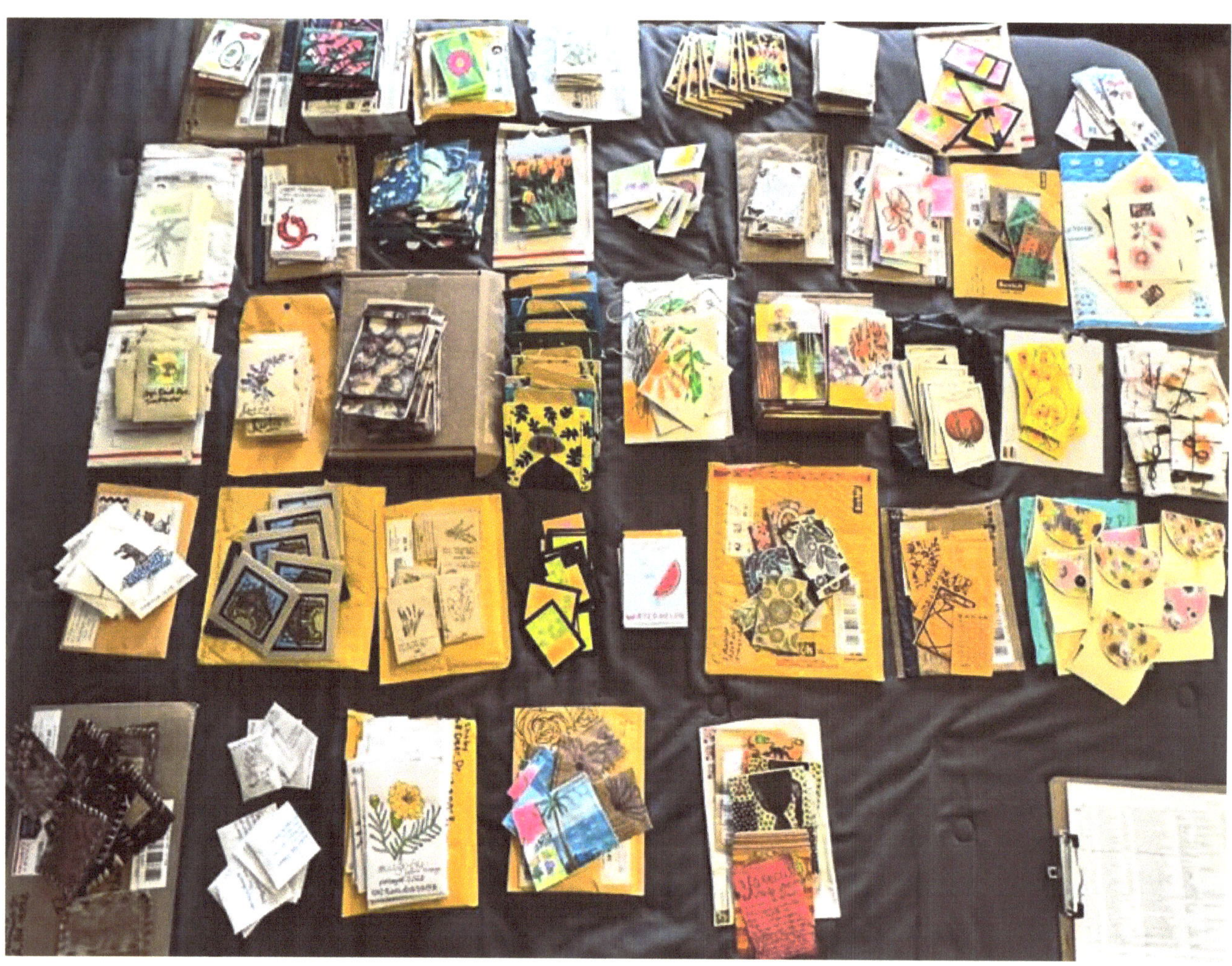

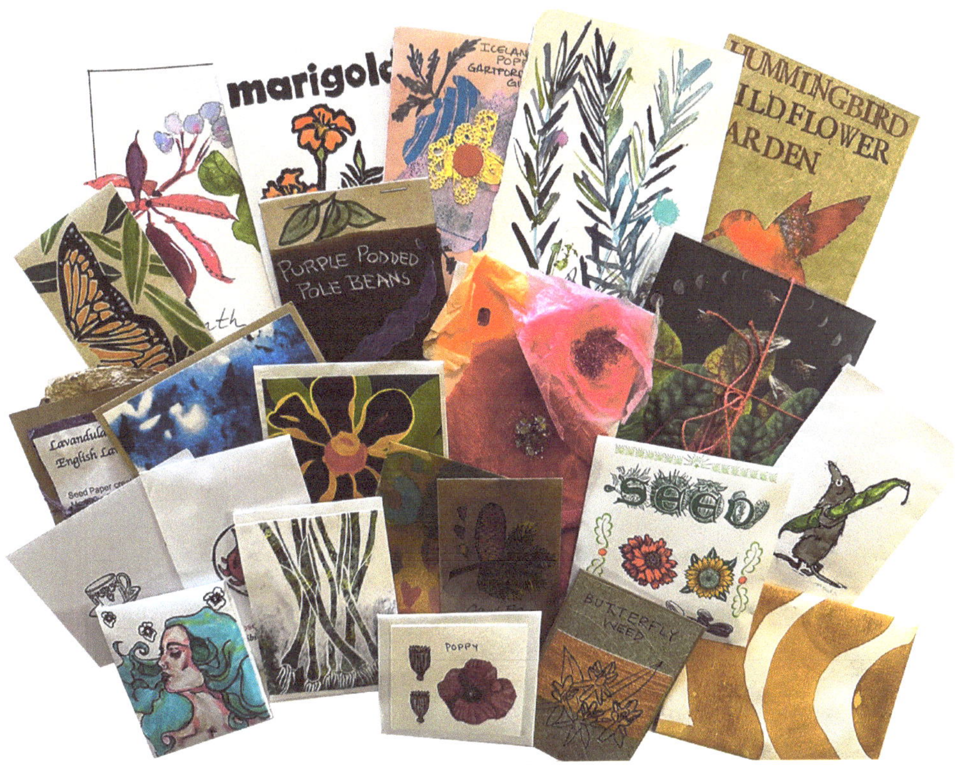
PURPLE PODDED POLE BEANS
seed
BUTTERFLY WEED
POPPY

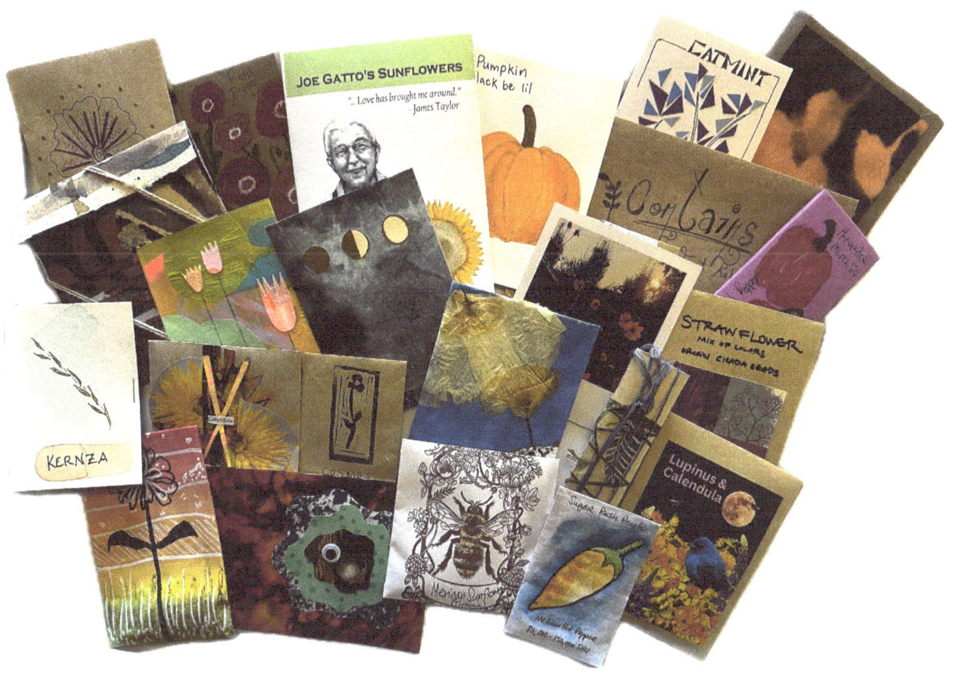
JOE GATTO'S SUNFLOWERS
"... Love has brought me around."
- James Taylor
Pumpkin
CATMINT
STRAWFLOWER
MIX OF COLORS
KERNZA
Lupinus & Calendula

Seed Sessions, our curated series of intimate gatherings, celebrates the fusion of nature and creativity. These thoughtfully designed events cultivate community through performances, storytelling, guest speakers, and hands-on experiences. They are spaces for inspiration, education, and connection, where ideas are planted, nurtured, and, like seeds, allowed to grow.

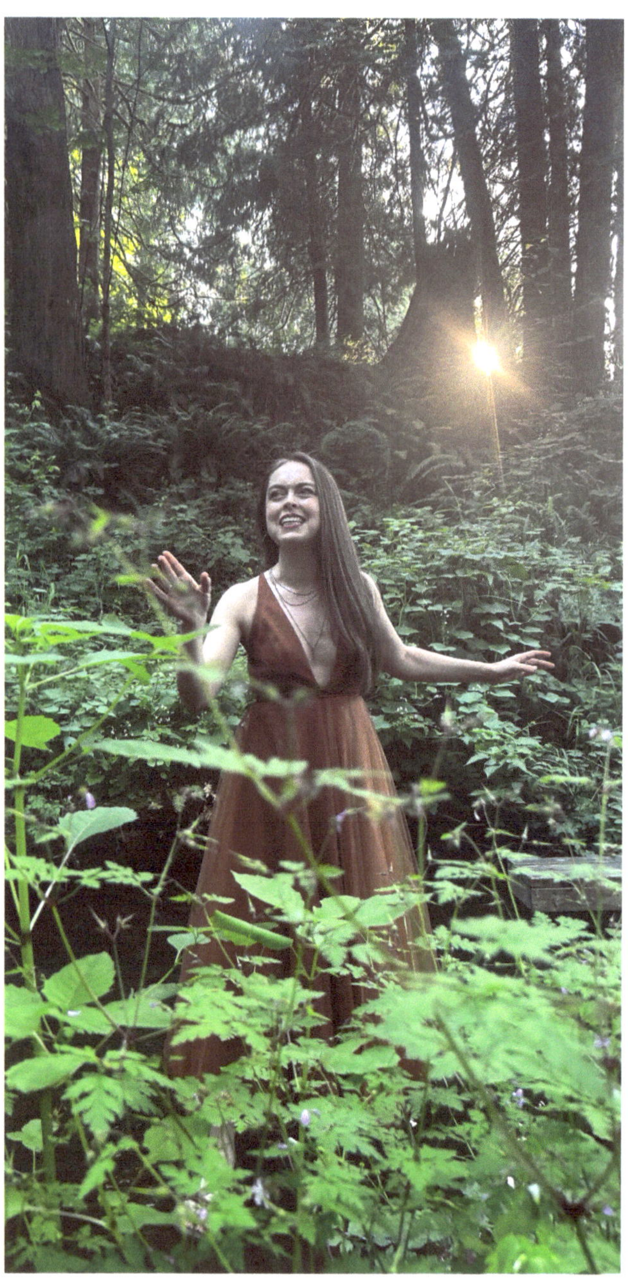

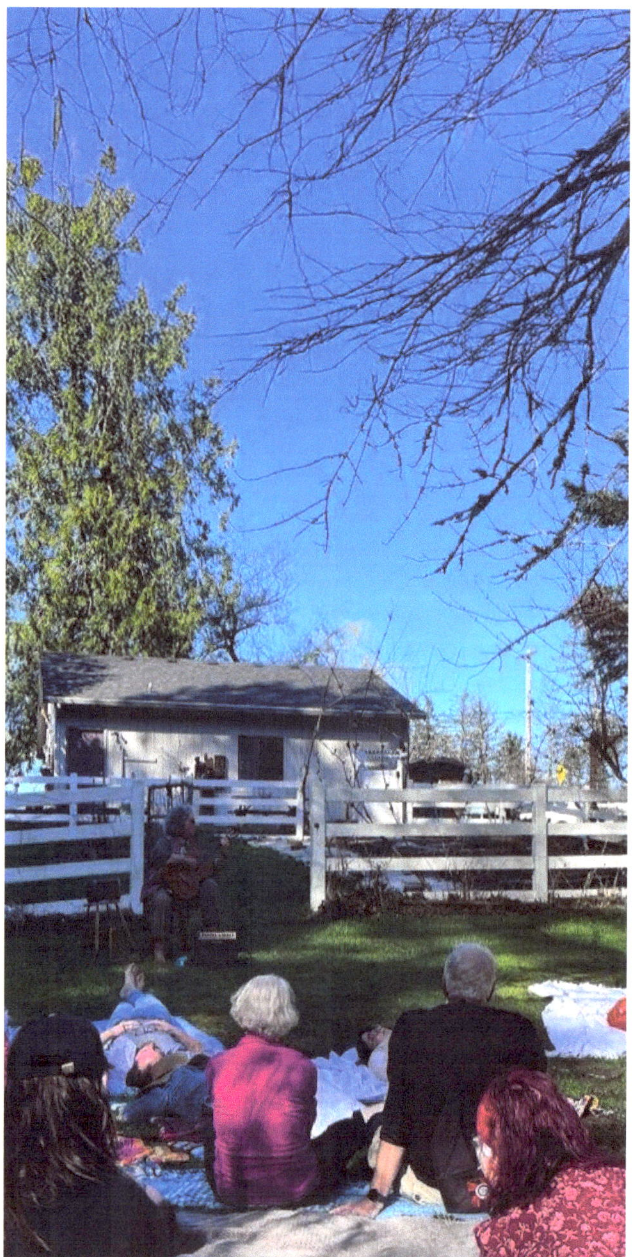

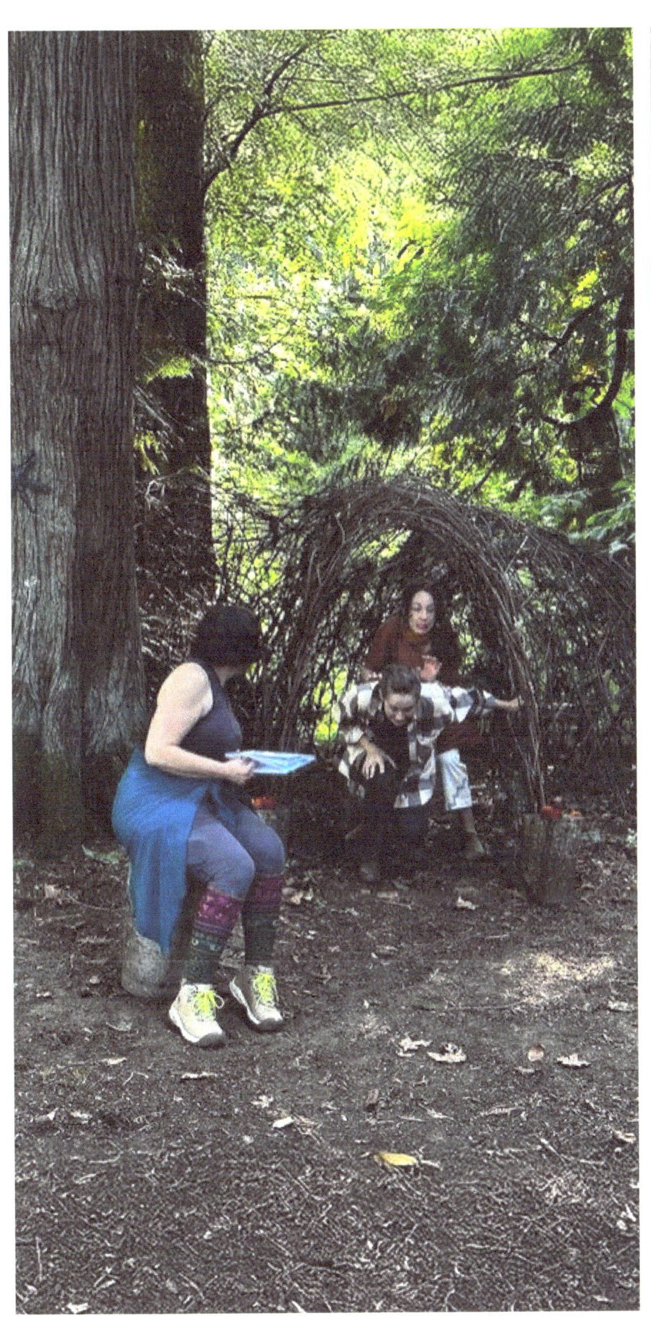

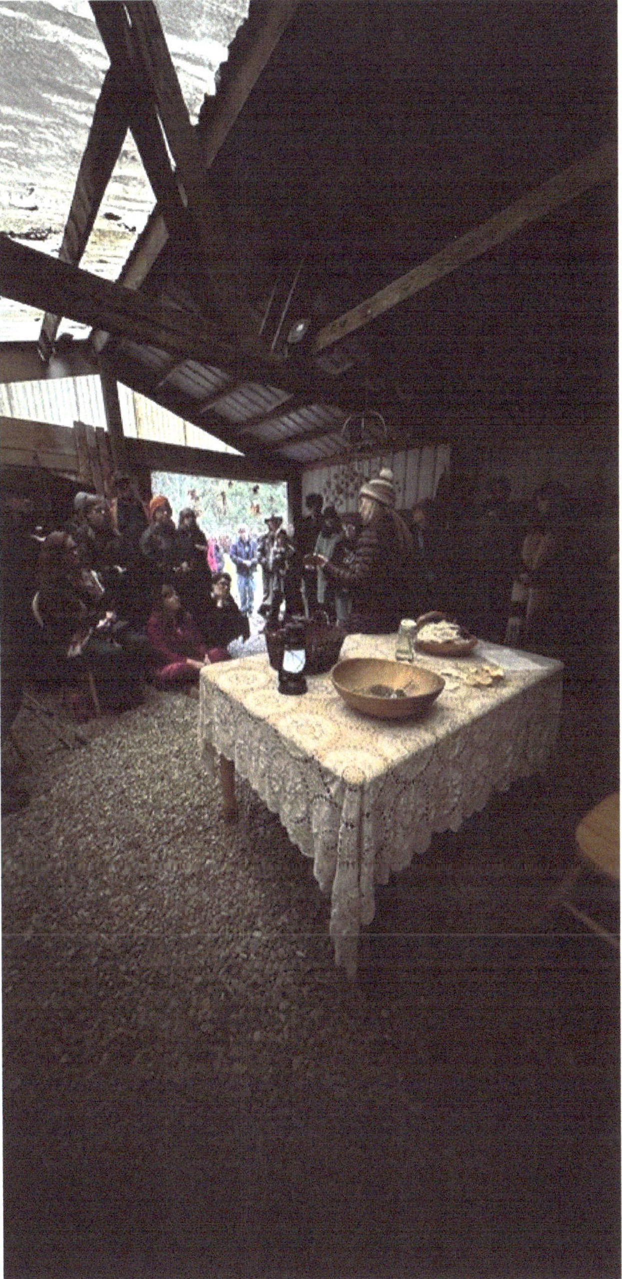

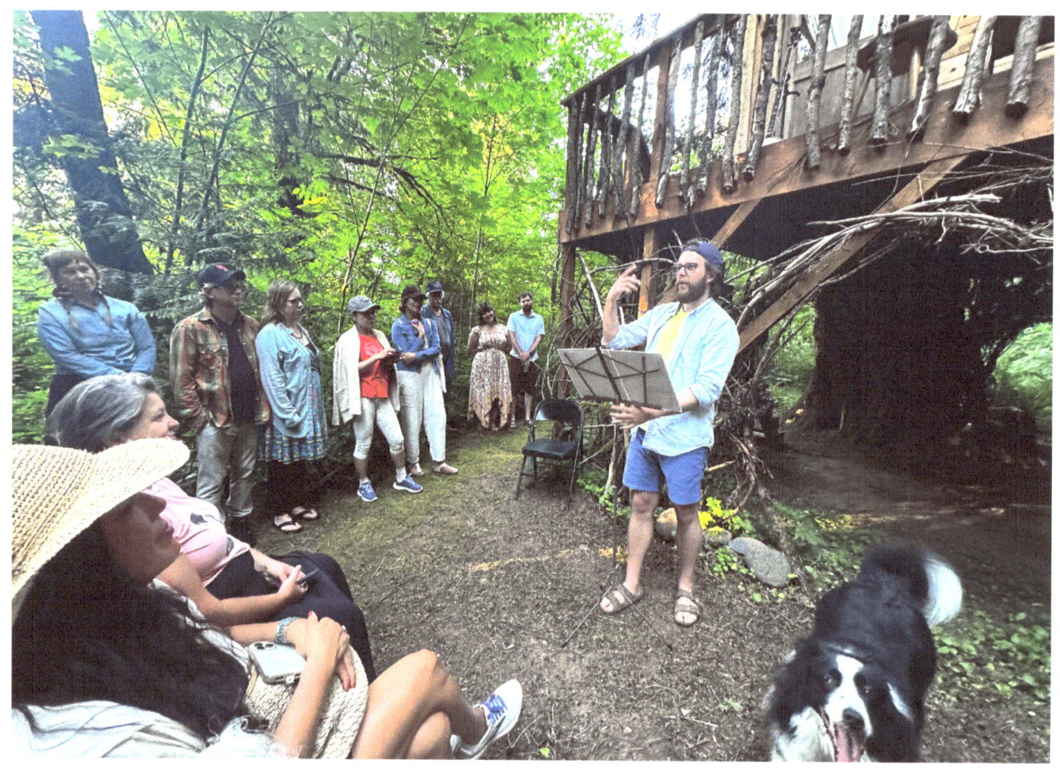

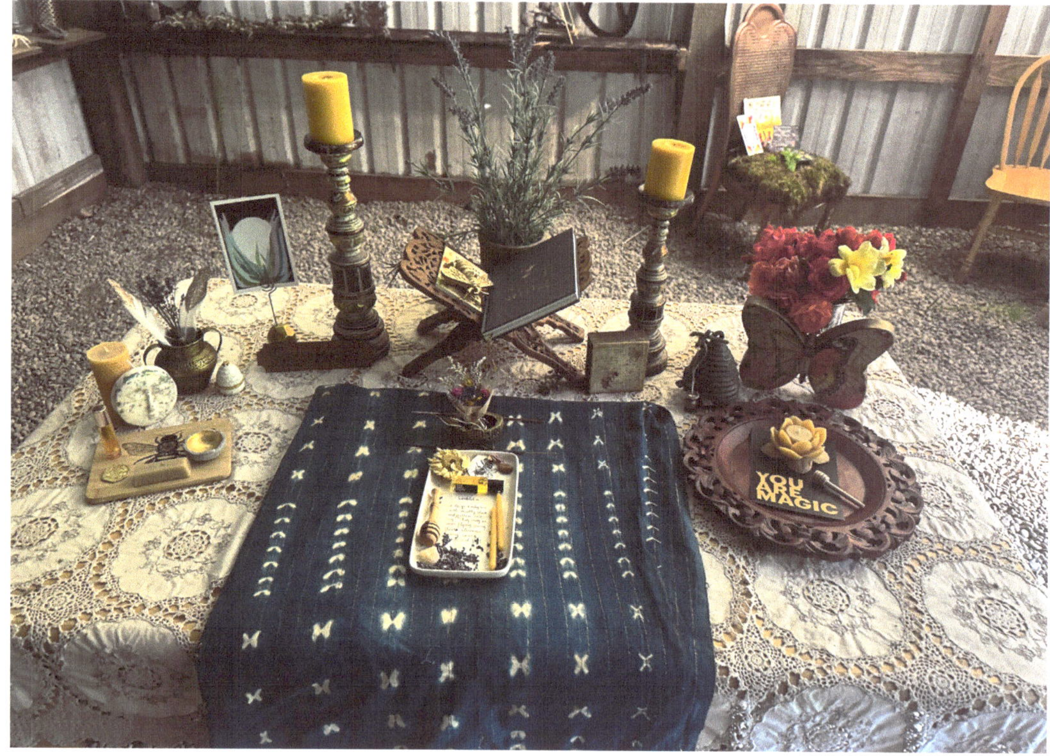
YOU
ARE
MAGIC

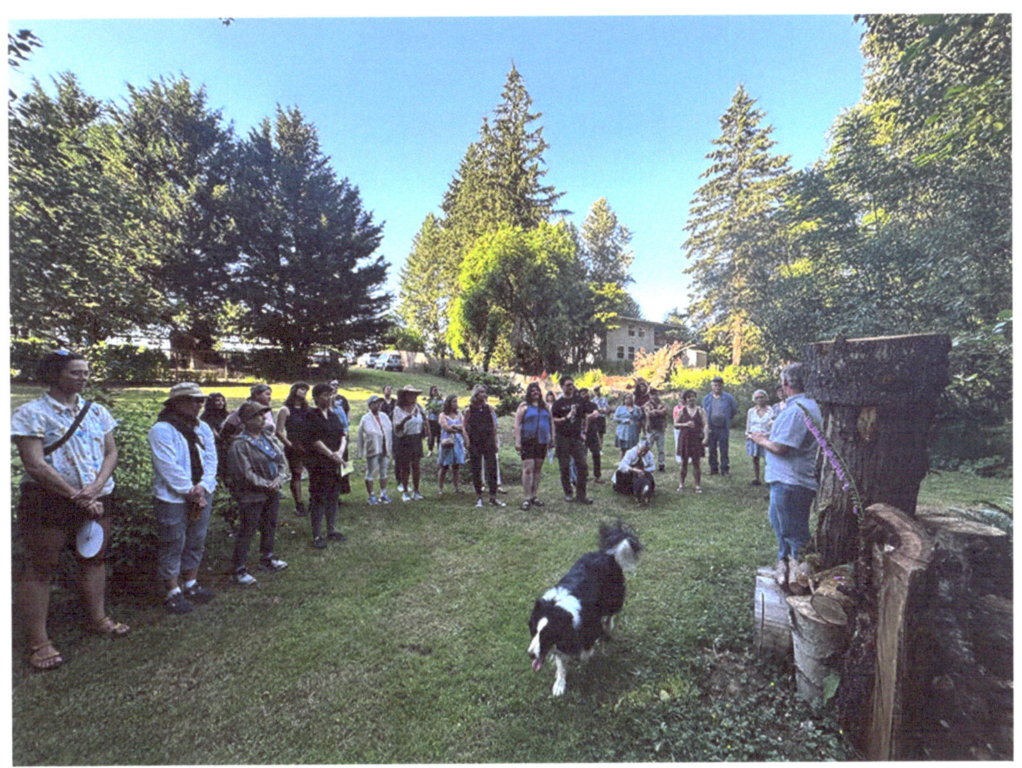

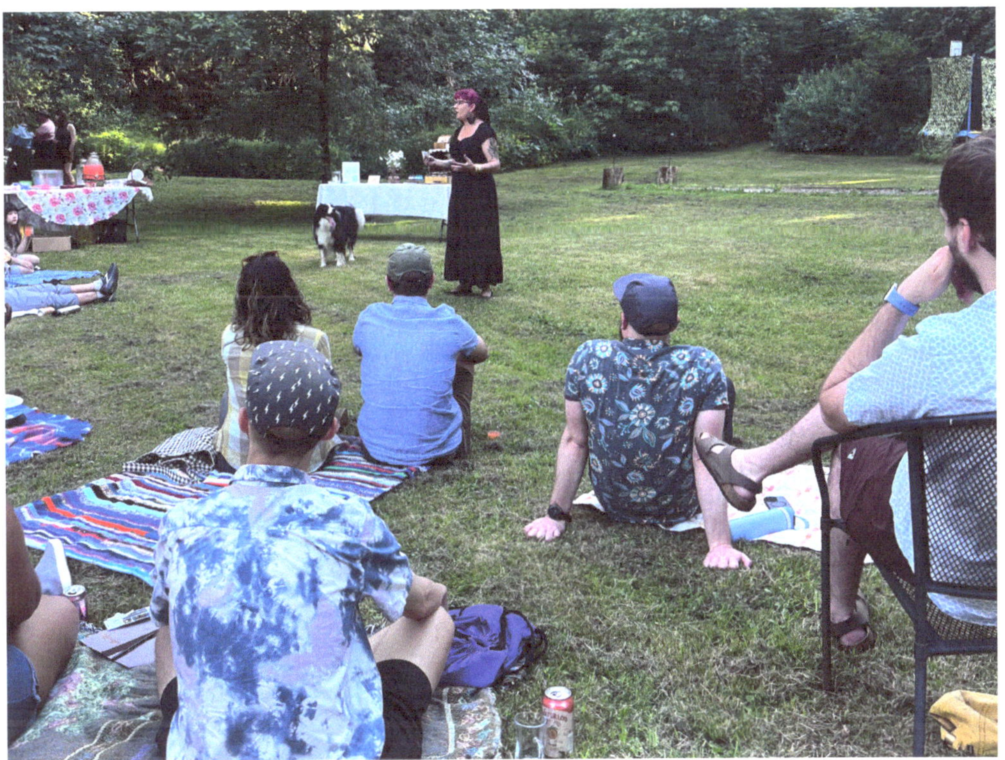

Terra Incognita, our site-specific land-art exhibition, was an extraordinary testament to the intersection of art, nature, and community. Over two deeply immersive weekends, twenty-nine artists and performers transformed the landscape into a living gallery, inviting more than five hundred visitors on a journey of discovery. Artworks and performances were woven into the woodlands, fields, ponds, gardens, and creeks, each piece in conversation with the land, asking us to see, listen, and engage more deeply with our surroundings.

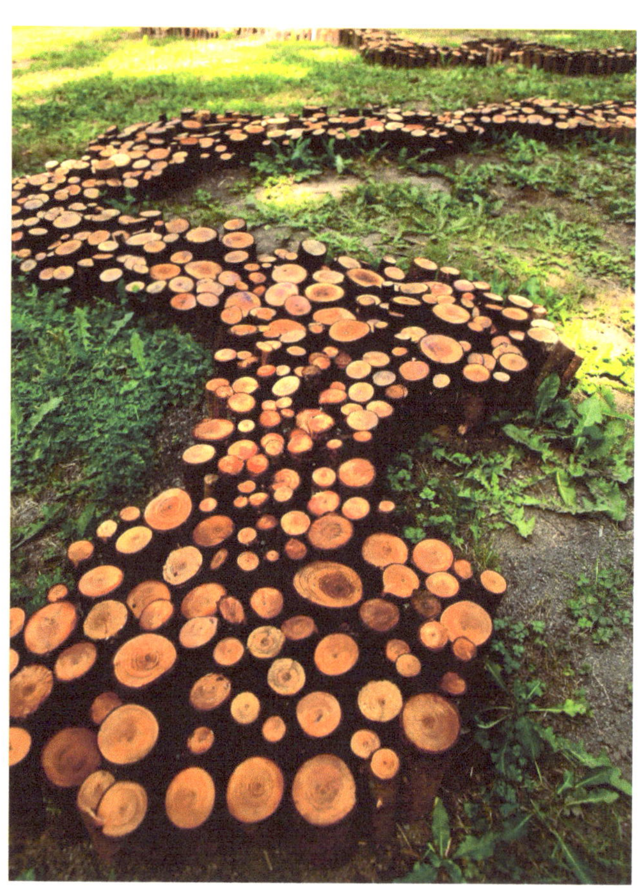

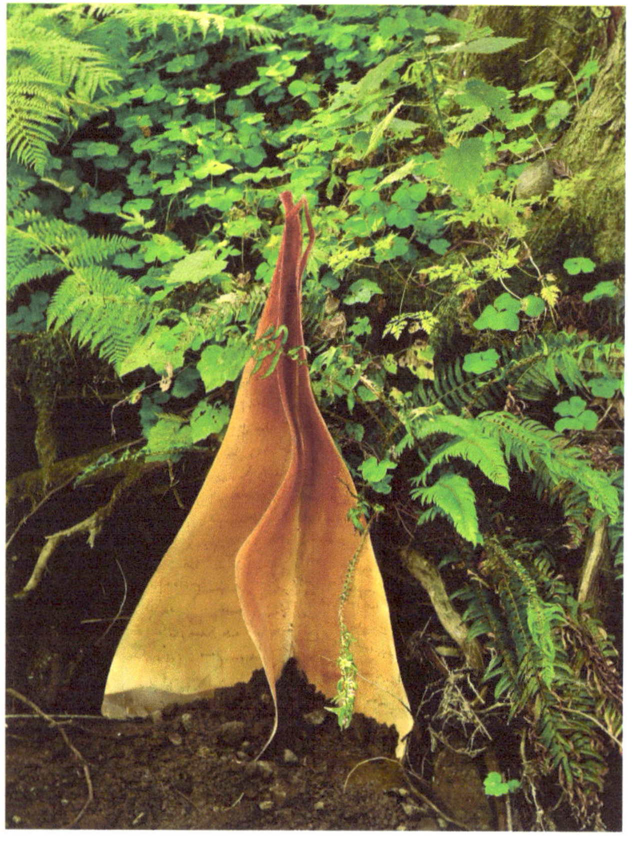

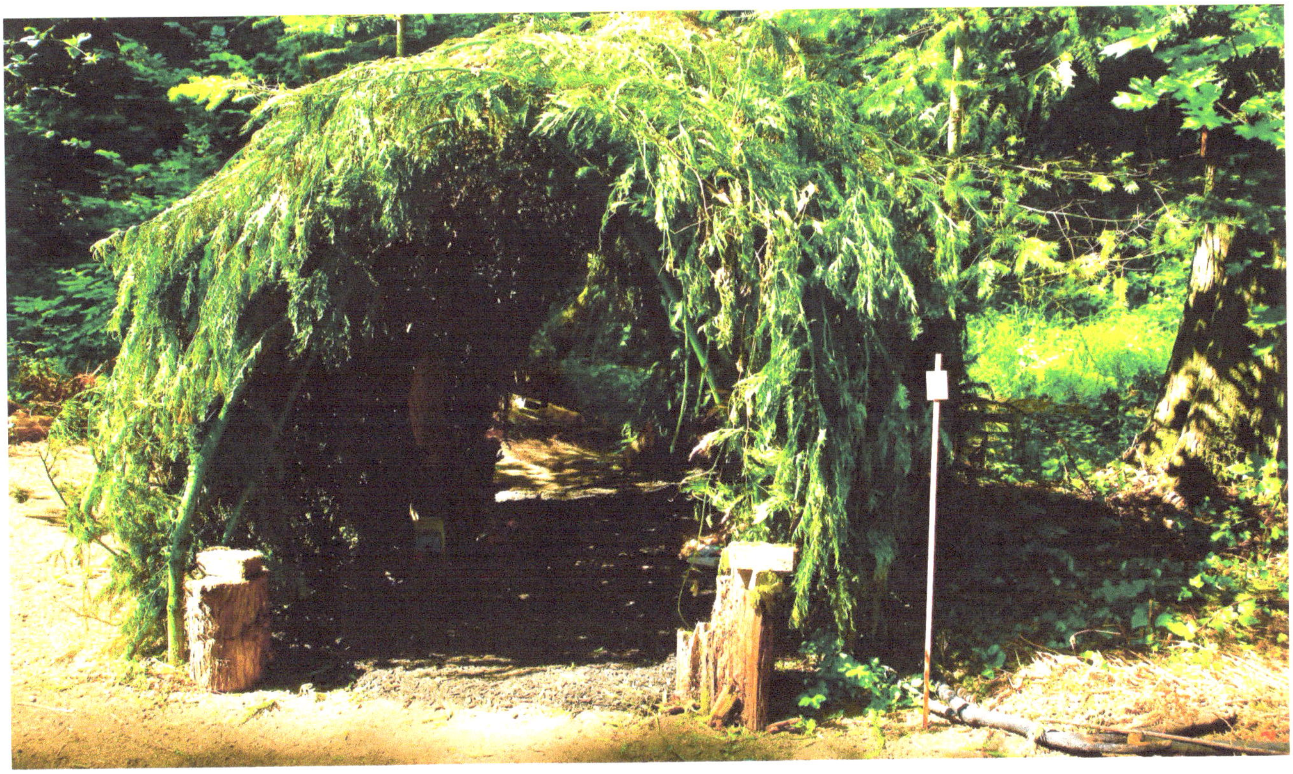

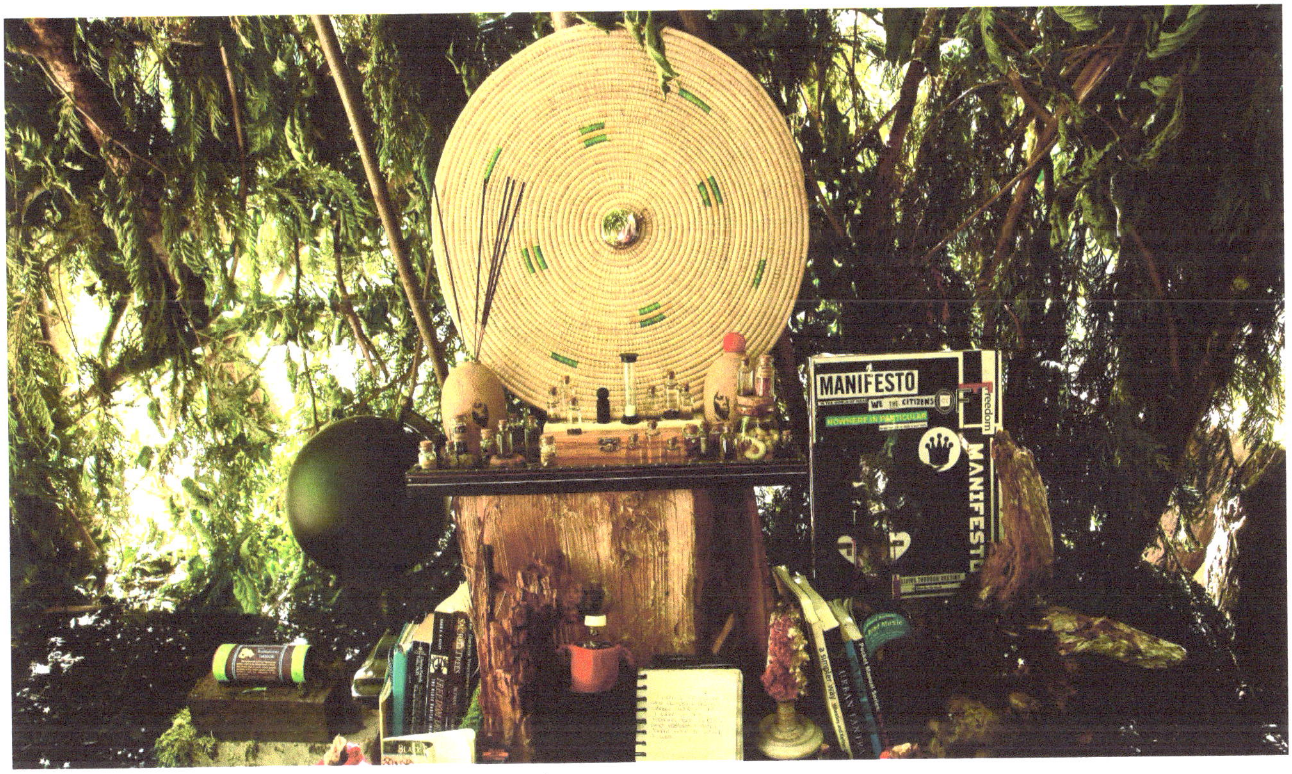

Scan to view video walkthrough of Terra Incognita

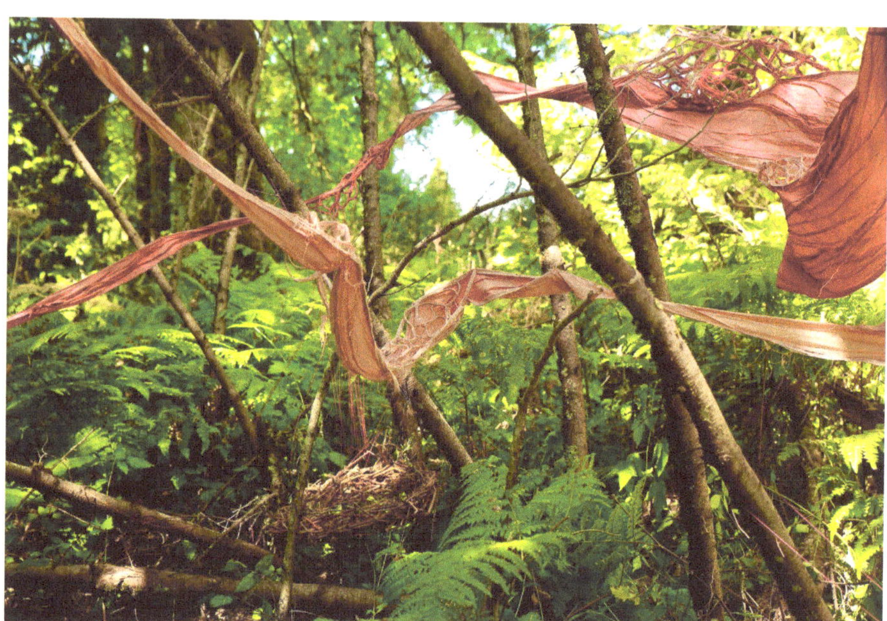

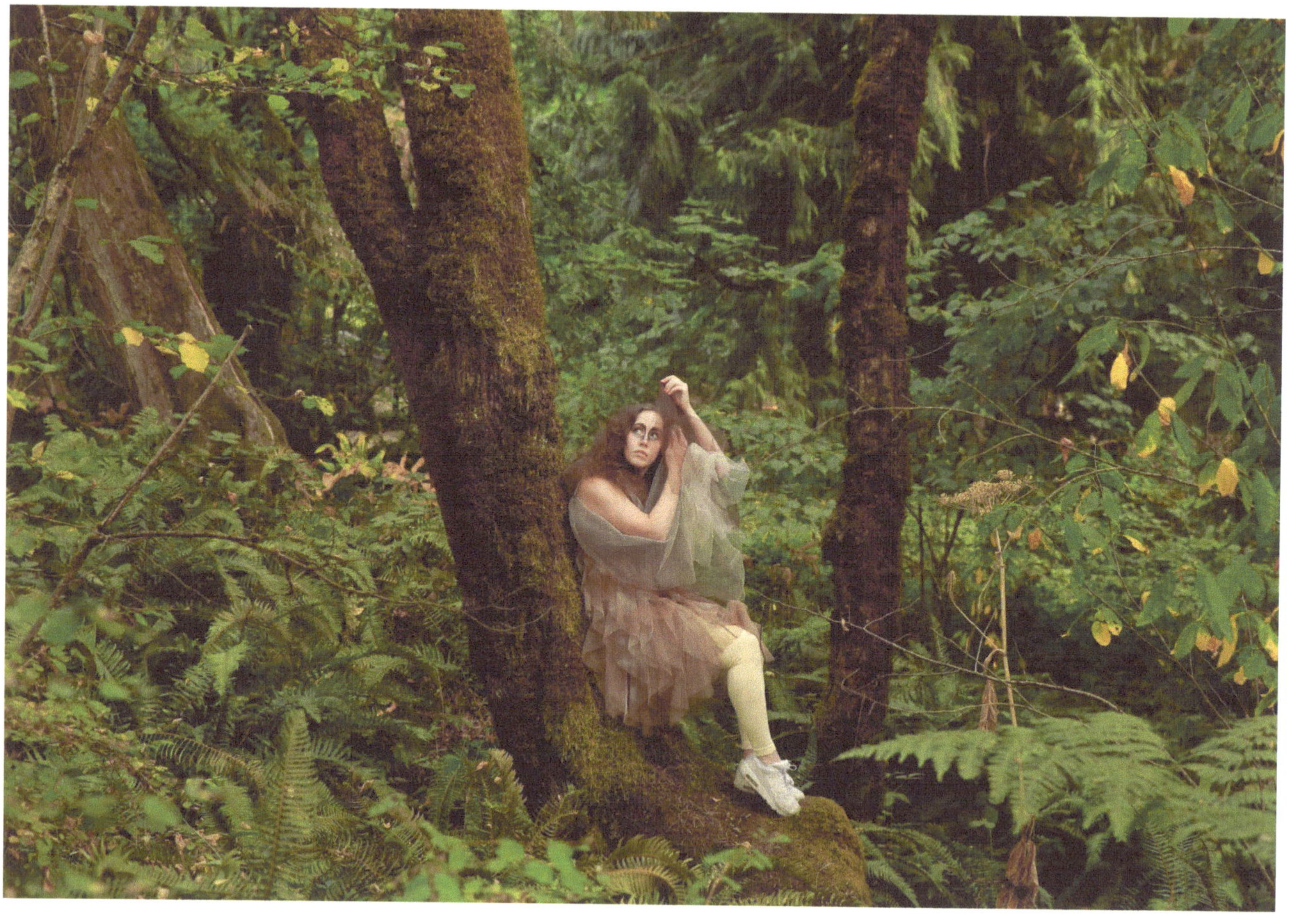

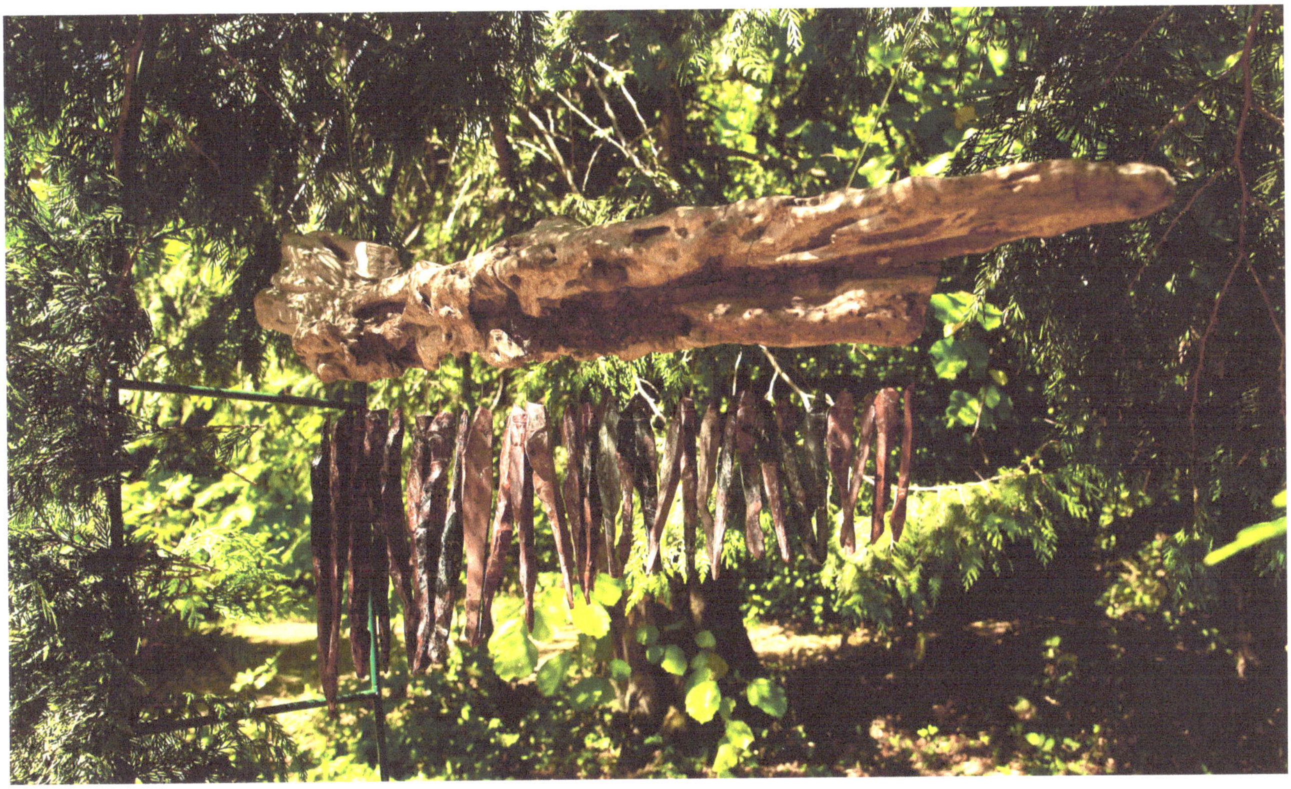

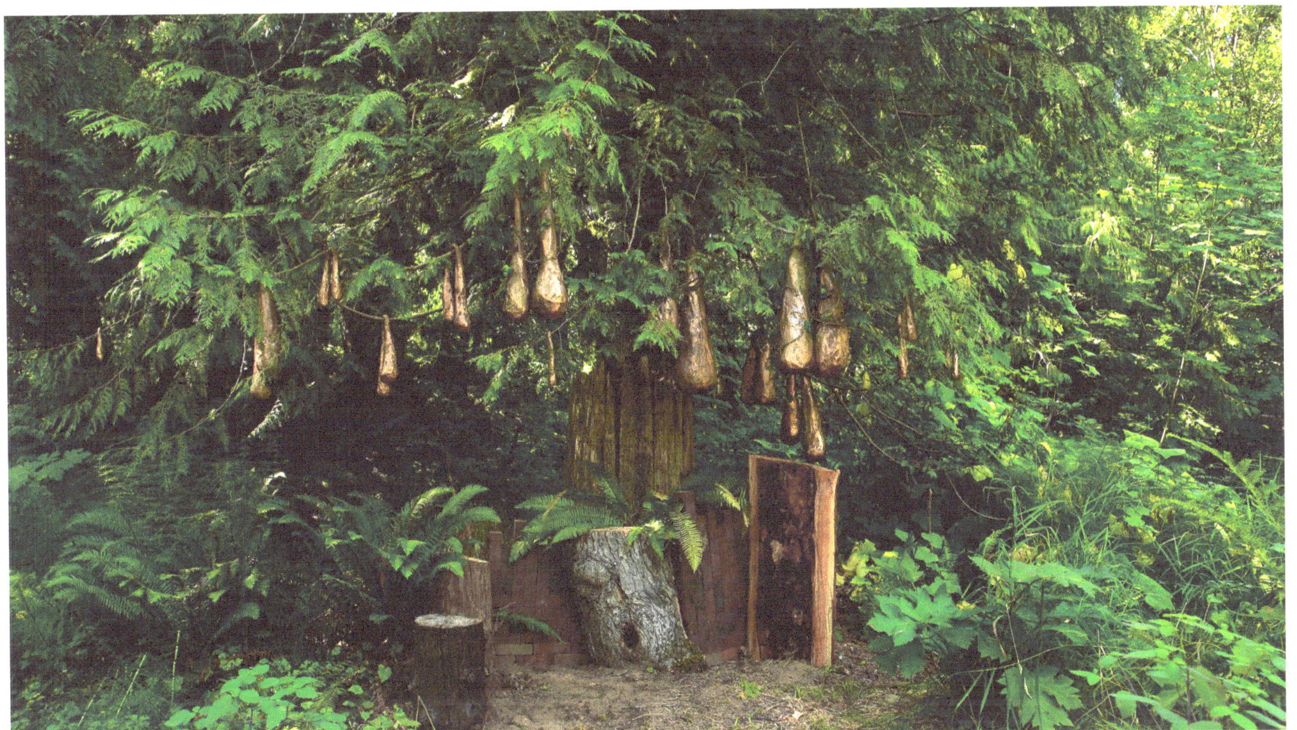

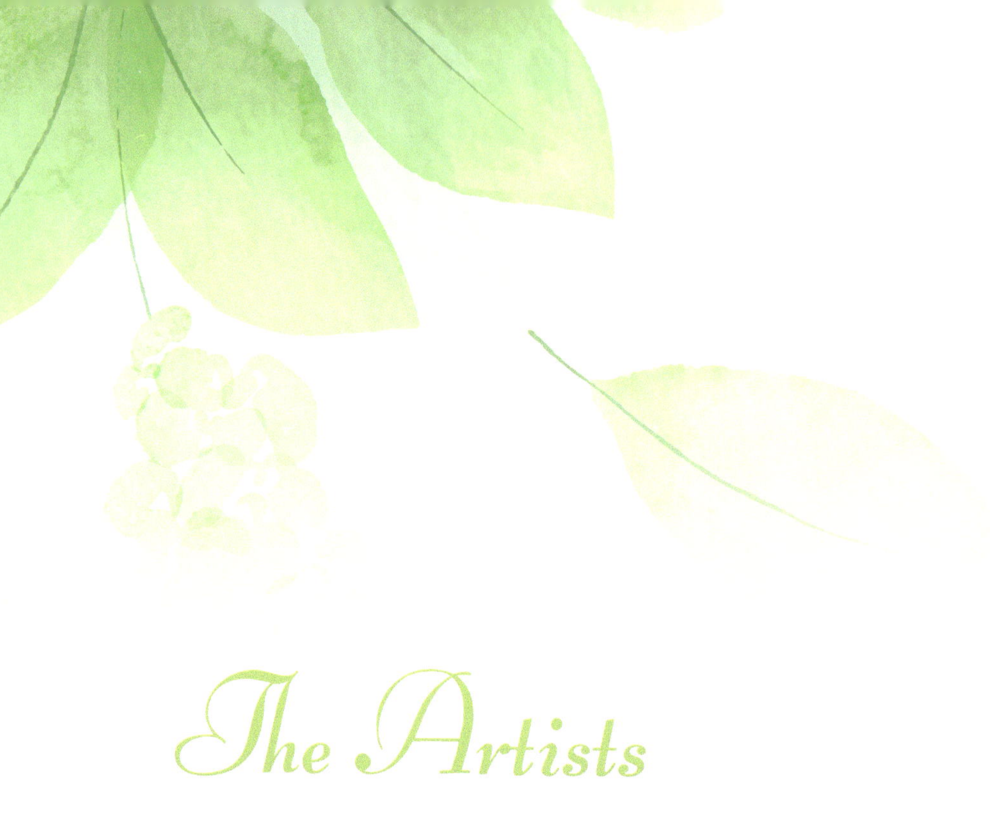

The Artists

Over the years, The Verdancy Project has welcomed an astonishingly diverse community of creative souls, writers, dancers, musicians, performance artists, poets, scientists, and visual artists working across every medium. Each one has brought their own unique perspective, energy, and curiosity, leaving something of themselves behind while taking something meaningful with them.

One of the most rewarding and illuminating parts of running The Verdancy Project has been witnessing the vibrant convergence of these disciplines. Creativity here feels fluid and alive, crossing boundaries, shedding labels, and sparking connections that often lead to surprising and meaningful collaborations.

But beyond the art itself, it is the people who have made this place feel so alive. These artists have inspired me in ways I never anticipated. They've challenged me to see the world differently, to listen more deeply, and to continually evolve as both a host and an artist. Some have become trusted colleagues, cherished friends, and even chosen family. Watching them create, struggle, rest, and bloom has been one of the greatest honors of my life.

I believe artists are essential to the health of our world. They interpret, question, translate, and transform. They carry truth and beauty, grief and joy, often in the same breath. They make the invisible visible and remind us of what it means to feel, to notice, and to care.

This land has held so many of their stories, and in return, they have become part of its story too. What follows is a glimpse into some of the incredible artists who have helped shape this ever-growing tapestry. Their presence and work have left lasting impressions on this place and in my heart.

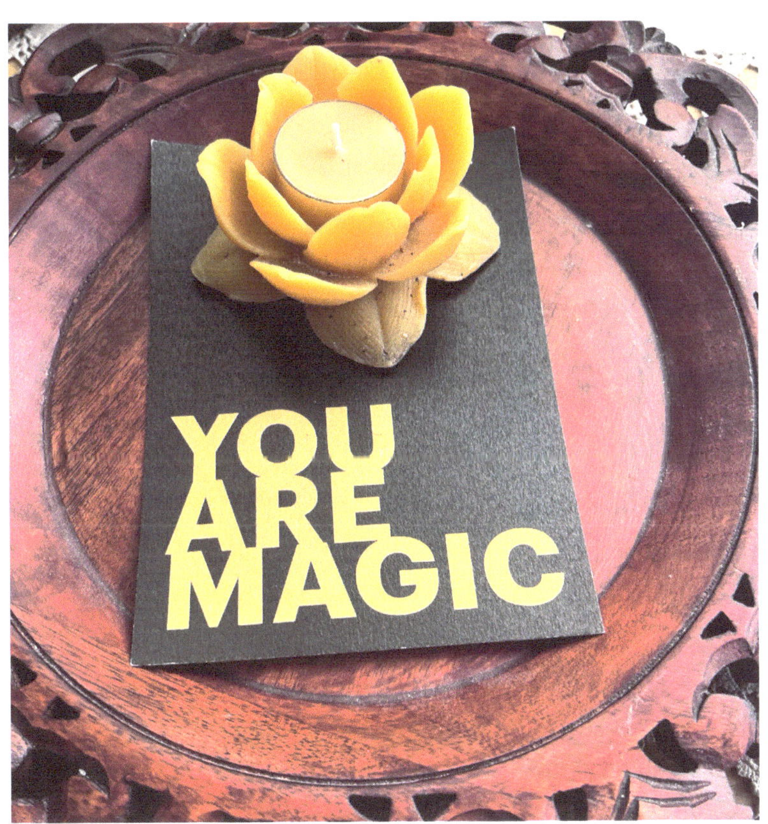

Brooke Kuhnhausen

The soft touch of moss. The music of water rippling over smooth stones in the creek. The trees breathing around and with me. The smell of fir and earth and sunshine on river rocks. As I work on my piece for the land art exhibition Terra Incognita, which I am calling Altars of Belonging, I place a river of vivid strawflowers and kelly-green moss into bark, and I feel a deep sense of meditative immersion, lost in this one moment of Kairos time. As I create surrounded by tree-folk at a wooden picnic table, adorned with flowers and bones, I am wrapped in a sense of communion and inter-being. On a piece of aspen bark, I write out the words of Joy Harjo asking us to "remember, remember." And here, at Verdancy, it feels easier to remember and feel that Earth-body belonging is so deep and we see how it grows stronger with our reverent attention. Here, there is a dear sense of being invited to co-create with the earth and also feel inside the Earth's dream, a sense of joy and possibility.

By the fire-circle, the gathering center of Verdancy, I feel the memories of fire-lit evenings, marked by laughter, song, and community presence in this earth-place. We savor the enchantment of seeing an opera performer sing out like a clear bell from the ripples of the creek, and a radiant dancer lilt and sway near a circle of ferns, delighted too as a snail crawls by, part of the audience and show. We tilt our necks back to soak in a storyteller, up in the treehouse, strumming his banjo and telling tall tales and we stand on a little knoll of green wild grass, with a piano nestled there, bathed in tales of Persephone. Tiny scrolls of poetry and word-magic are opened up while tea brewed from the garden is sipped. Some evenings we let the stars rain over us, murmuring in shared awe and wonder.

Every step on this land is a sense-memory of earth-connection, communion, and co-creation—the heart of Verdancy joy.

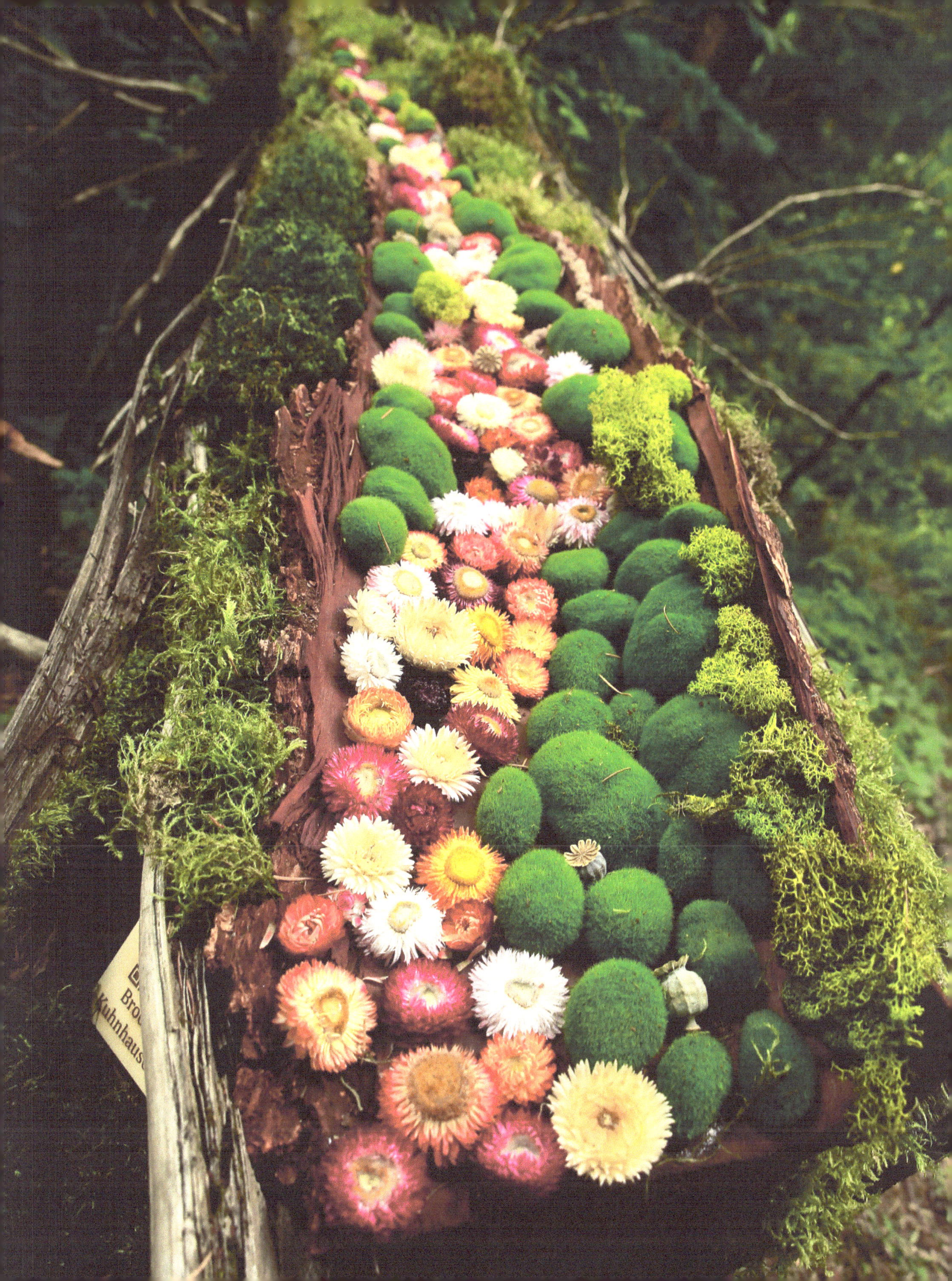

Joellen Sweeney

One of the most powerful lessons I've learned from TVP is how letting go of my expectations around productivity and "shoulds" frees my creativity. Every residency, I've had almost the same rhythm: the beginning is a flurry of doing, doing, doing; the middle is a crisis of faith ("Do I even know how to make art? Do I stink at this? Are all my ideas basically worthless?"); the climax is the promise I make to myself that "today I will make nothing" and then the denouement is a few days of easeful, joyful, surprising creativity. And those days are such rich soil—I end up experimenting with media and ideas I've never touched before, which may not come back to visit my professional art-making for weeks or months or ever. But the refreshment of that kind of creative play, without expectations, is so nourishing.

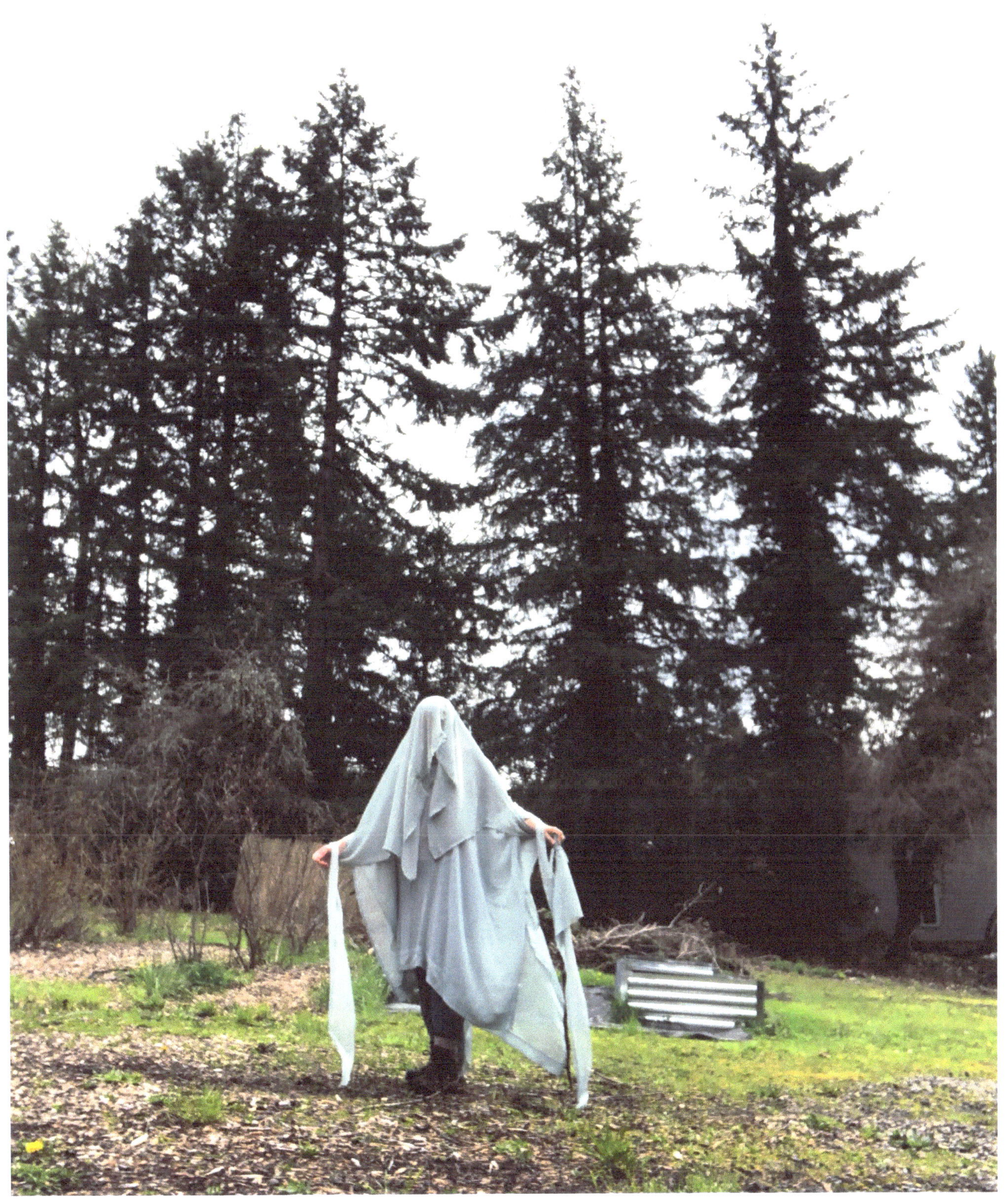

Joellen Sweeney

Ravings of a Wayward Bogwoman, an EP of Verdancy Project Songs

I've been lucky to participate in TVP's residency program each year since 2021. Every time I go out to the land, I bring a whole mess of gear: keyboard, mic, tripod, notebooks, colored pencils, two to seven books I mean to read, swaths of diaphanous fabric, a handful of very loose ideas. I've learned from experience that this is the way to enter the woods—repared but open, available for any wild eventuality. The ideas that visit me at TVP are never the ones I expect. A theatre-artist by training, I find myself wading in the creek with handcrafted puppets, jotting down poems in my sketchbook, or (most often of all) writing nature-inspired songs that I mostly don't share with anyone. *Ravings of a Wayward Bogwoman*, my little EP, is a selection of some of the tunes I've written and recorded onsite during my residencies. Each one was completed in a single session, and they are full of the images and feelings that captured my attention on my daily wanderings: the milky blue of the swirling water, the raucous screeching of chickens, the feeling of weight lifted off my shoulders in the shade of tall trees. I hope you enjoy!

Scan to listen

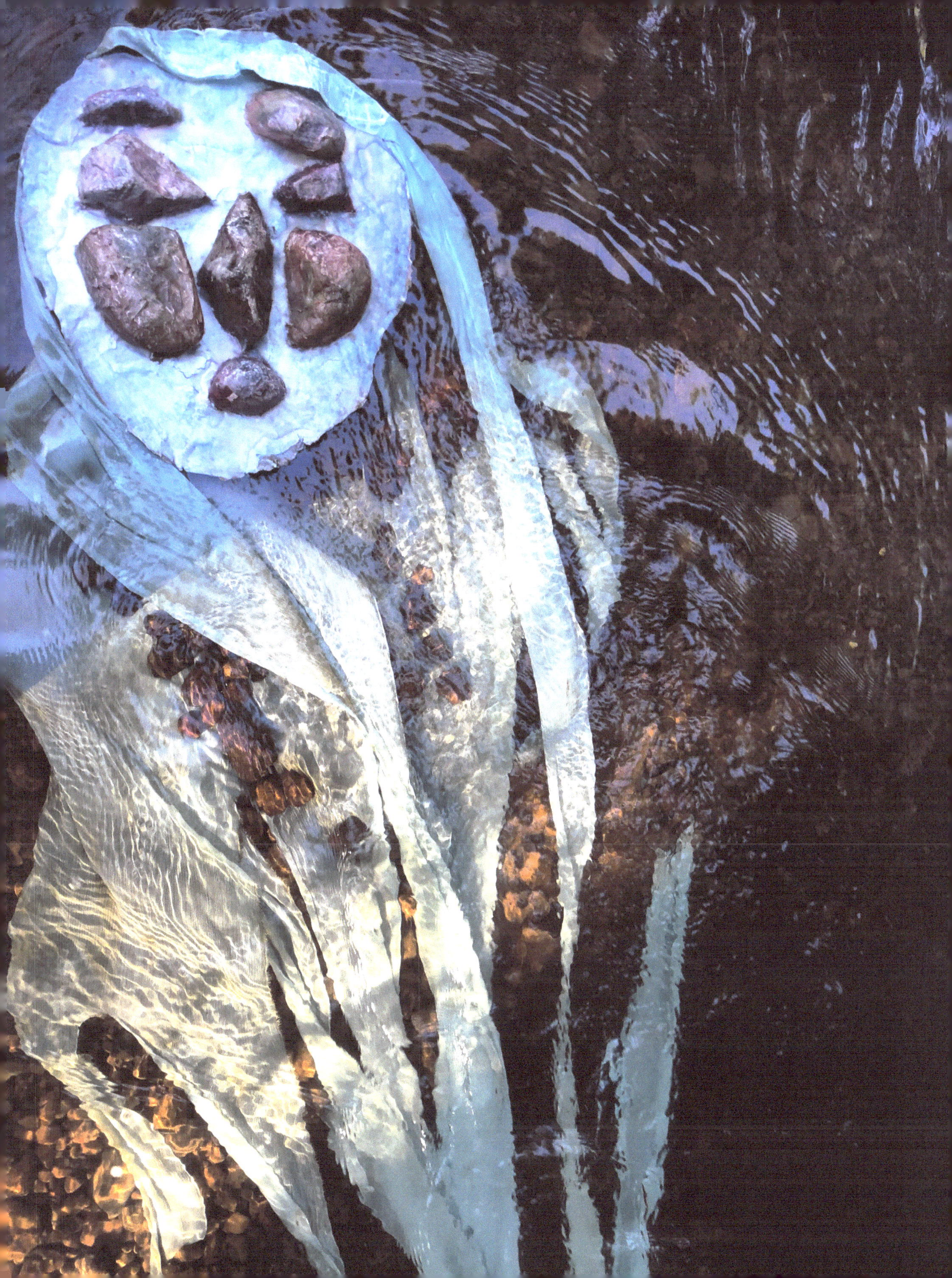

Brittney Corrigan

The first time I walked through the grounds of The Verdancy Project, I couldn't stop uttering the word *magical.* A tiny reading room: magical. A beautiful mural overlooking an abundant garden: magical. A library of nature's many offerings: magical. A home for busy bees. A whimsical caravan wagon. A hidden treehouse. Magical, magical, magical. I felt exquisitely lucky to have been invited to read my poetry as part of an autumn equinox Seed Session and honored to be a guest on such lovingly tended land. Sharing my poems with a wonderful group of humans while standing beneath the branches of the key tree by the creek? Yes, magical. And as I walked the paths to listen to the songs and performances of the other artists, I felt transformed by the power of art and the comfort of community. I carried the magic of those creations, of those connections, with me as I left The Verdancy Project that day, feeling hopeful that these types of shared experiences will keep our hope lit in these dark times.

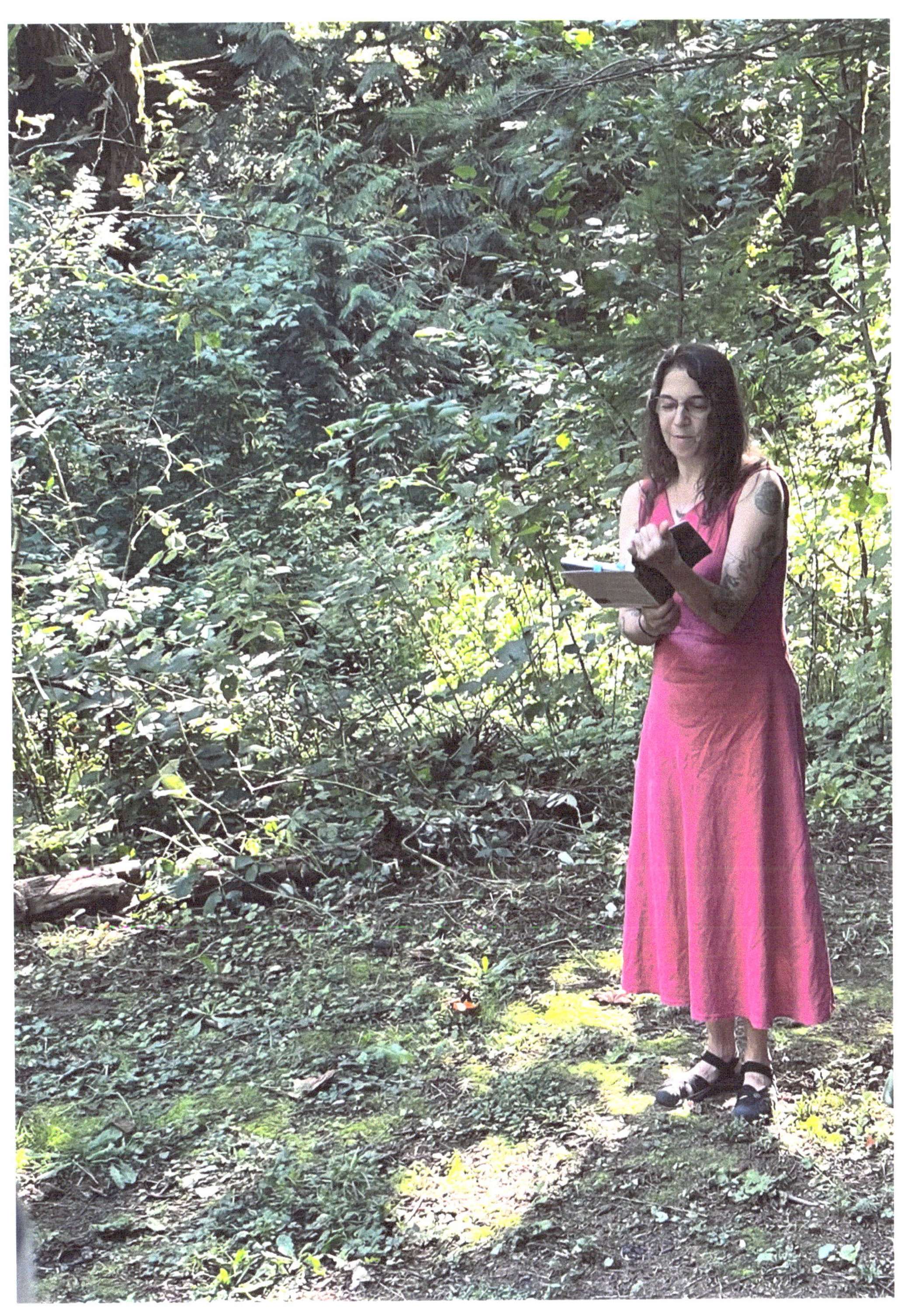

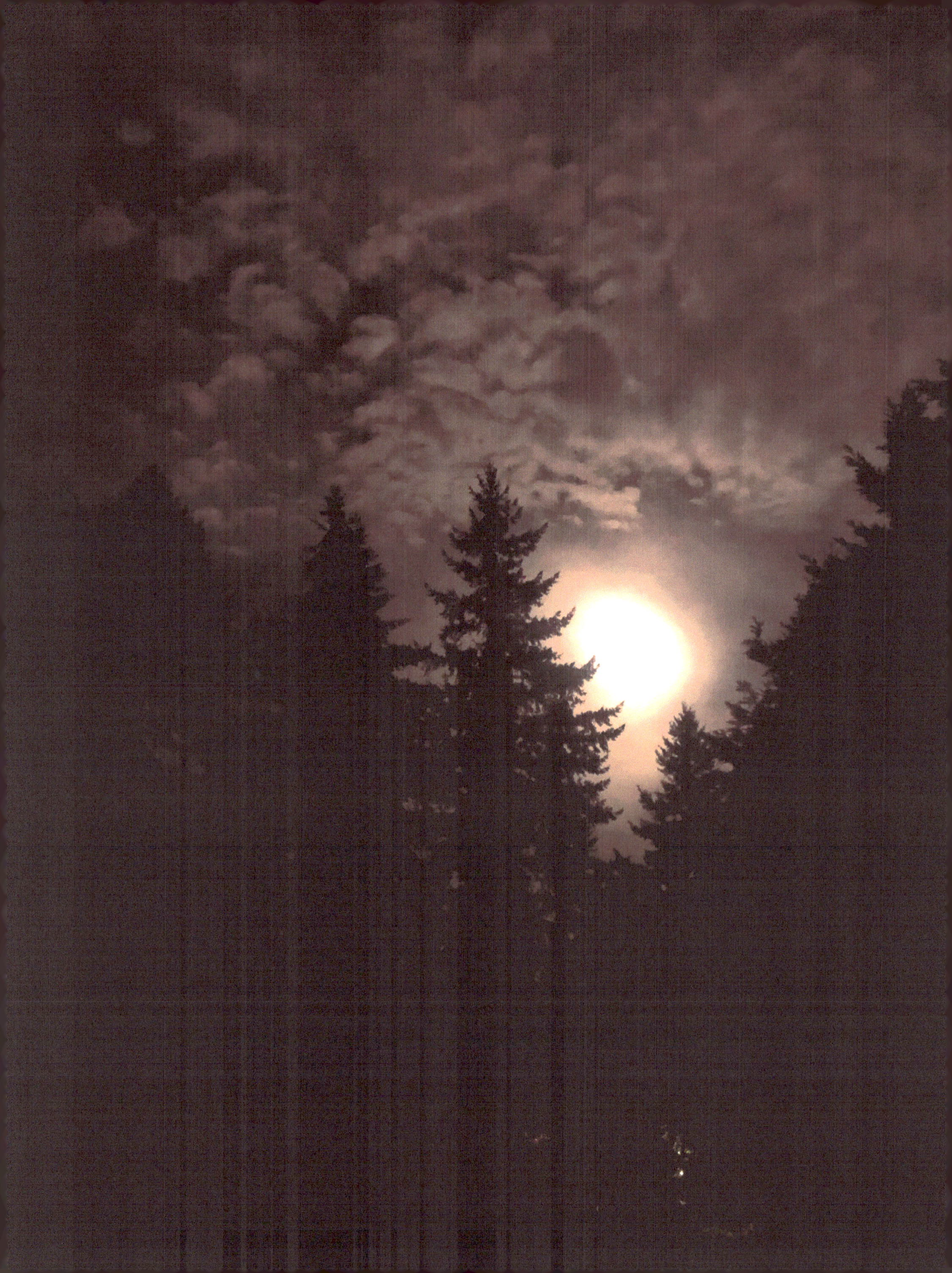

Brittney Corrigan

All Your Stars Are Out

After a line by J.D. Salinger &

after Robert Procter's "Starry Starry Night"

after Anne Sexton's "The Starry Night"

after Van Gogh's "The Starry Night"

Water holds spirals of time, blue froth of change against land that goes deep, tells stories with rock and bone. The green season turns, blazes in the dark. Where land meets sky, the unknown riots with life. The night is not empty. It swirls with the eyes of tiny gods. Though light left these stars thousands of years ago, *they are all alive*. The writer's heart is alert as the wind-tilted beachgrass, as the incoming tide. The poet sifts, wonder-dappled, and finds herself among small beasts. The painter dots a brush against earth to bring down the stars. The artists converse in fertile color, death suspended between them. The century-wide canvas waxes and wanes. Land blends to sea blends to sky, an unconformity of elements. One golden moon splits to bright orbs of many moons. One blue crest becomes a village of stars. The silence brims layer upon layer, lustrous. Time is swallowed up.

the world is alight

creation of heart and mind

all your stars are out

Linda Robertson

My time at the Verdancy Project was one of the most productive of my two-decade-long art career. The beauty and diversity of the land, ease of access, and freedom from distractions was a perfect combination for me. I was almost immediately inspired by new ideas, and they continued long after I left.

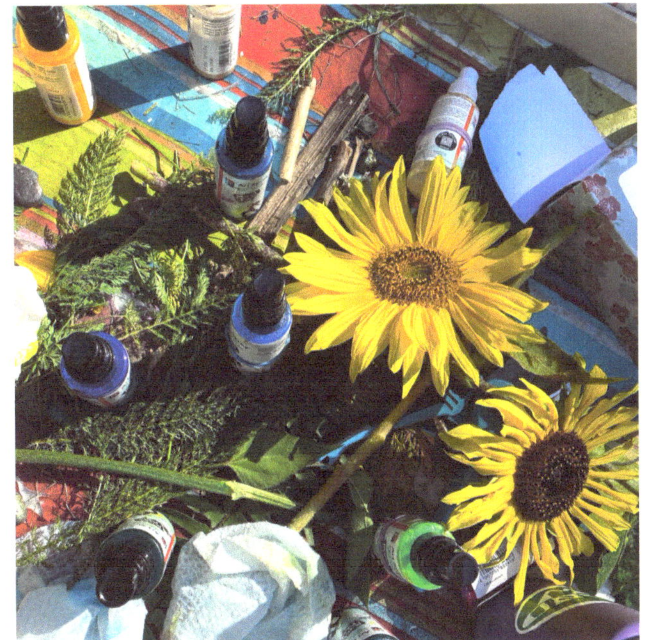

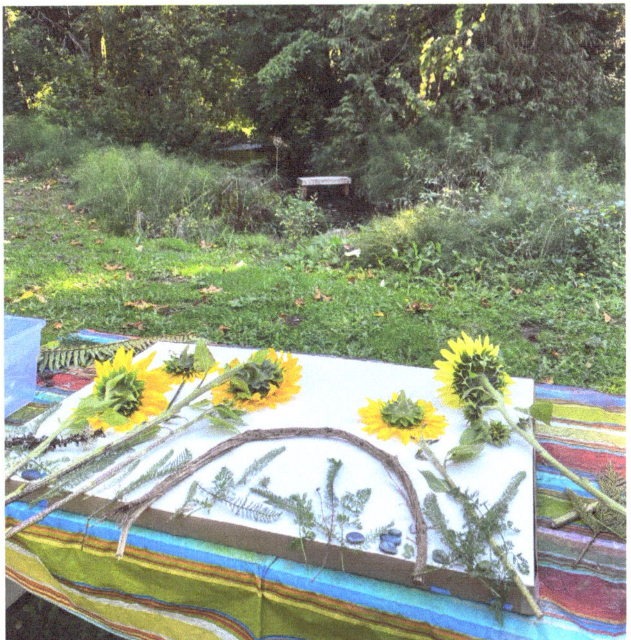

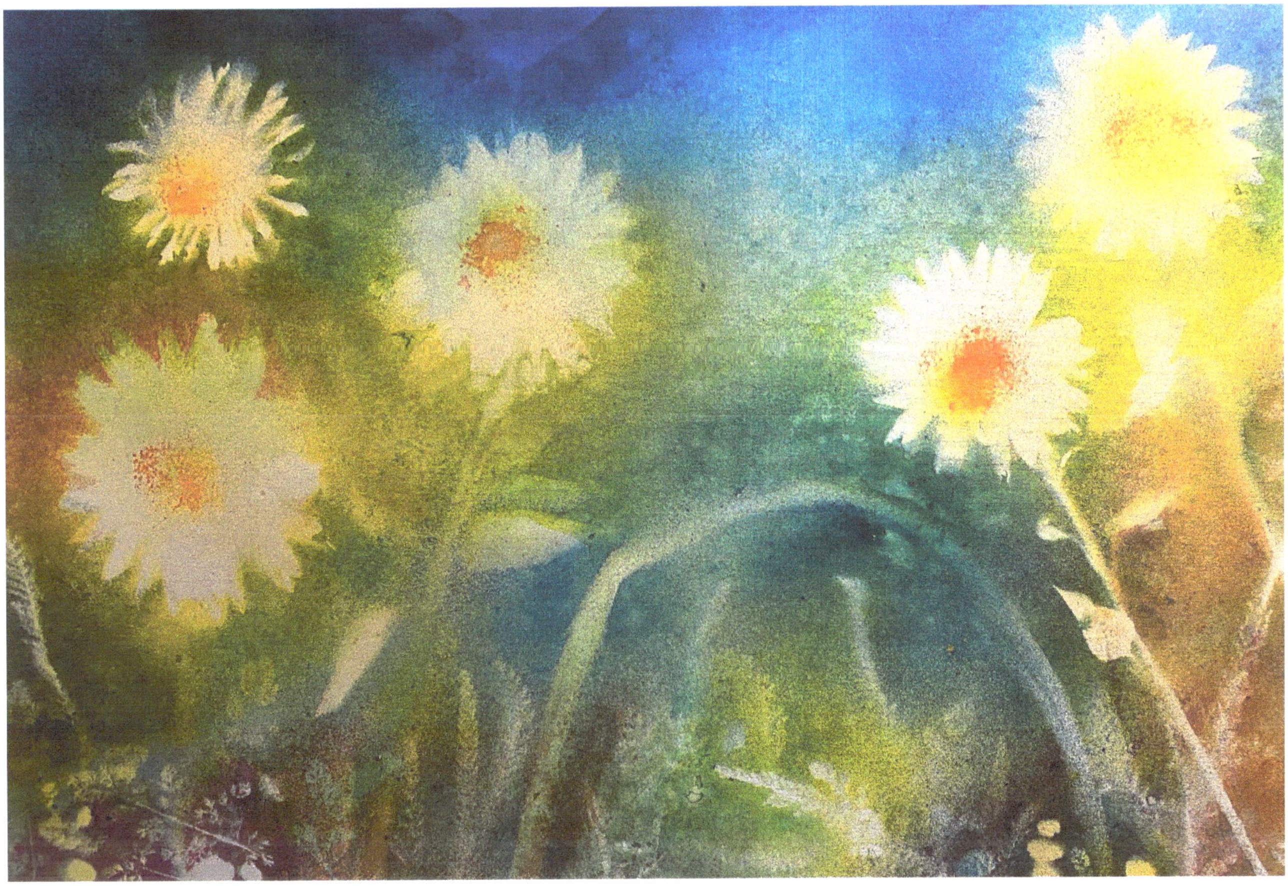

Rose Covert

I created my first land art piece at The Verdancy Project. Getting to step onto the land and conceptualize the piece with the land itself as a reference point and collaborator deepened my relationship with the land aspect of my work. I got to interact with the trees, birds, bugs, and dryness of the soil as the project went along. I got to feel myself connected and part of the land as I worked directly into the landscape. It allowed me to dream in a new direction and take my work further than I had before.

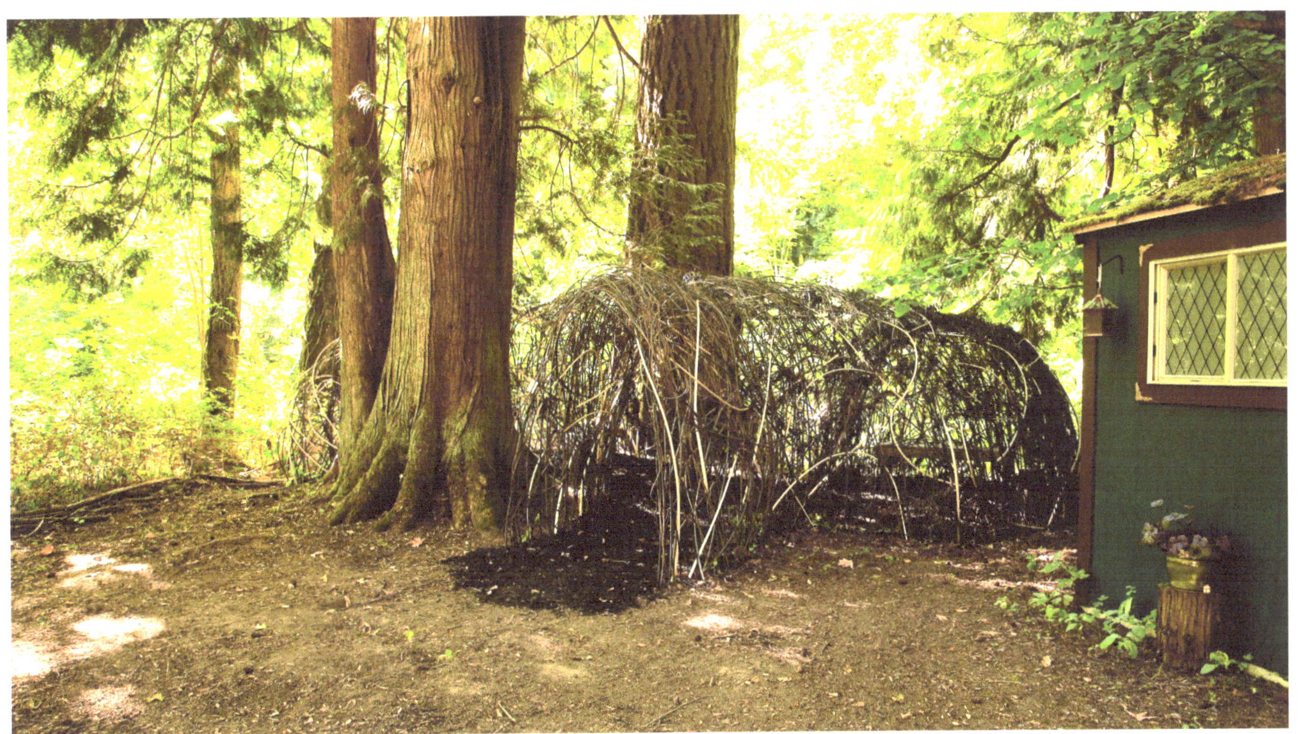

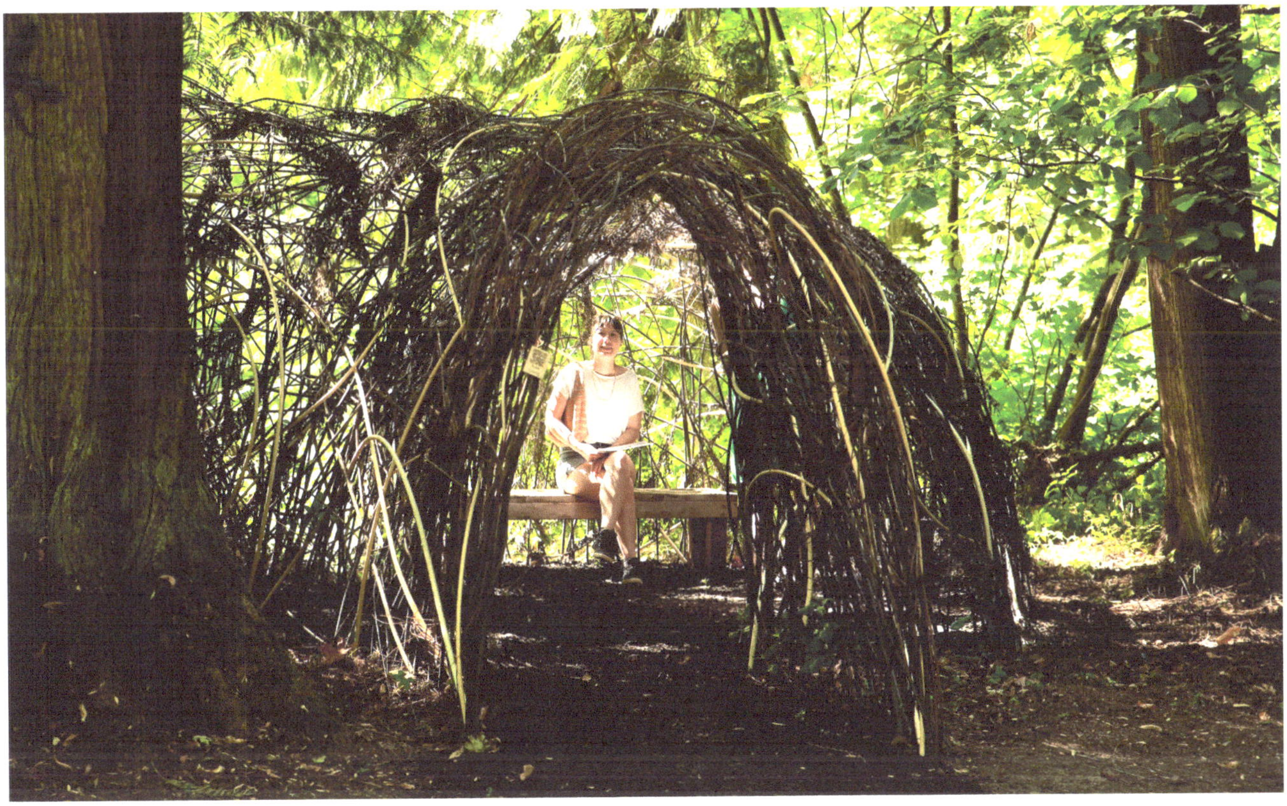

Rose Covert

I think exploration is the feeling I carry with me from my time at The Verdancy Project. I got to explore and discover so much while working on this project. I was in a process of discovery the entire time. I have carried this sense of stepping into the unknown and playing my way through it with a mind to exploring as I go.

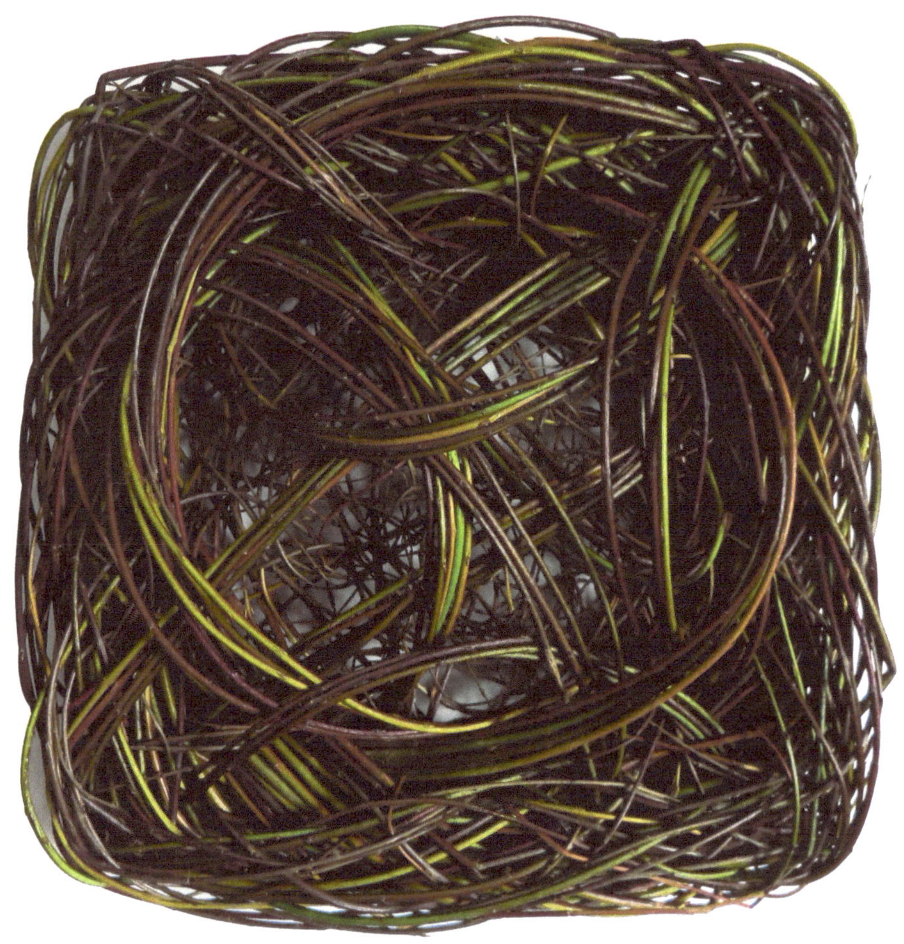

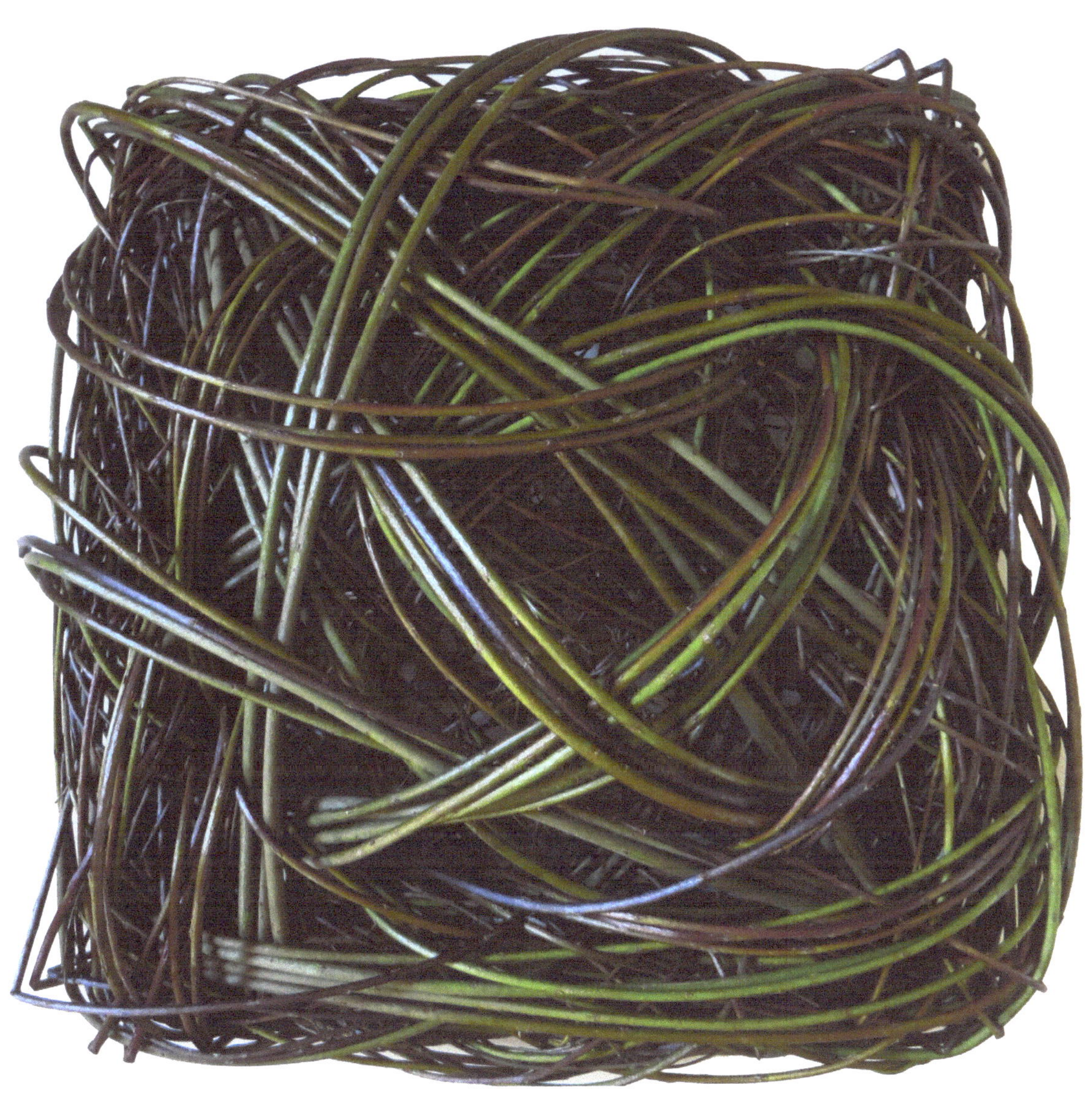

Anna Czoski and Sabin Timalsena

We extensively draw inspiration from natural systems in our art practice; by augmenting nature we can highlight beauty in its complexity. For this installation, Sabin generated a procedural animation of concentric circles shaped by a depth map that Anna created to trace the woven geometry of willow branches. The animation was intentionally simple so that the concentric circles converged along a pathway within the sculpture, both highlighting the volume while flattening the surface. The sparse and hypnotic animation, when overlaid on the dense natural forms, revealed details otherwise imperceptible.

To view the animated projection-mapped installation: scan the QR code and launch the augmented reality (AR) web app. The photo will come alive with a video overlay.

Scan to watch
an AR video

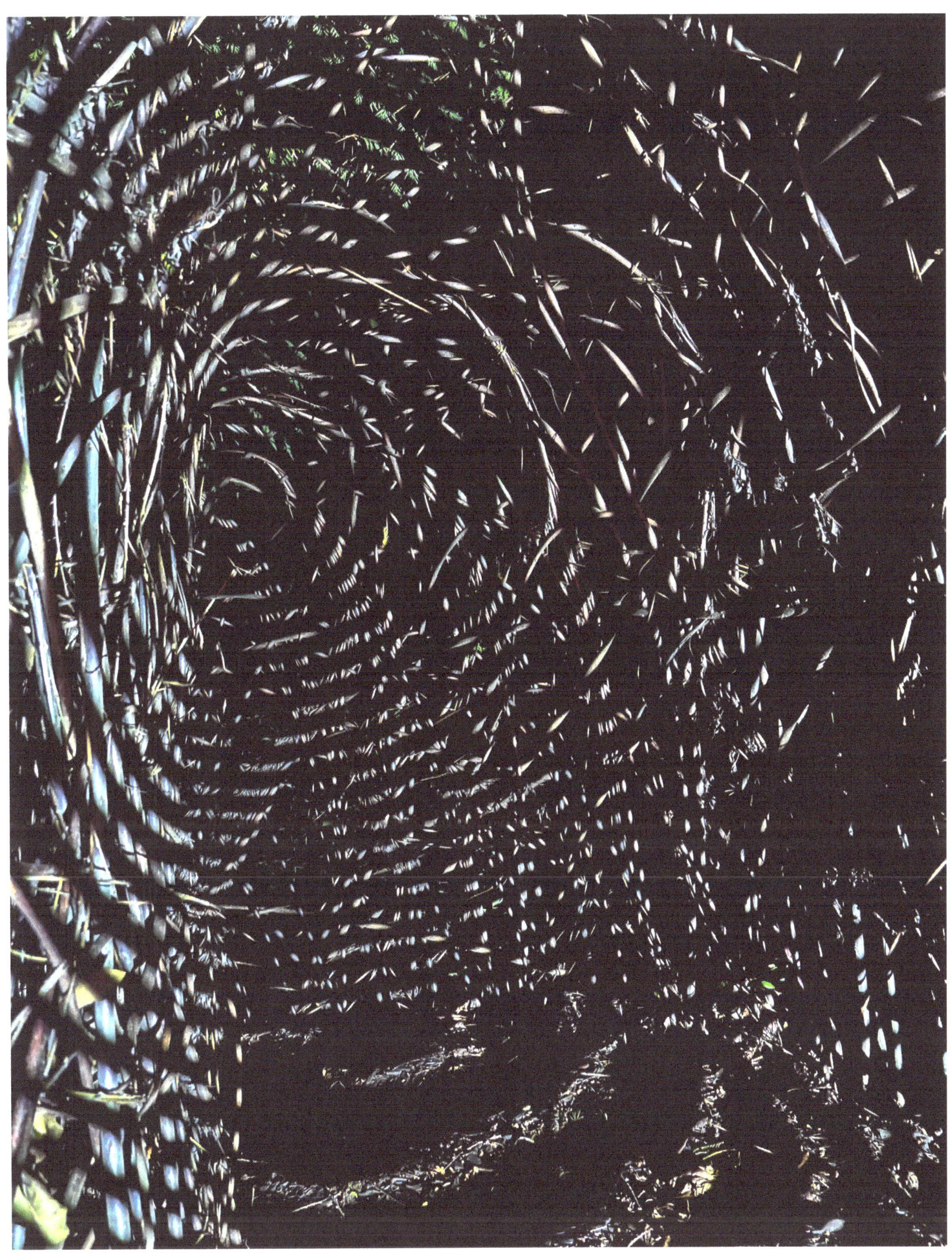

Conor Eifler

The House Under The Tree

Barmy Norbert had been acting barmy. Even for him.
I don't remember being a kid, says he, d'you?
Me, I don't remember what I done yesterday, and I tell him as much.
Same as me, says he, you swabbed the deck like every other day. Whatchoo think the rum's for?
I've forgotten.
Exactly, says I. We drink to forget. That every day is just like the day before.
I don't remember anything before.
There weren't nothing before.
Surely there was.
Nothing worth remembering.
I think that's the end of it, but then Norb tells me he's of a mind to find his treasure.
Where'd you bury it? Says I.
Don't know, says he.
Didn't you make a map?
'Course I did.
Where's that?
Buried that too, didn't I?
What'd you do that for?
Can never be too careful, says he, there's pirates abound.
He had a point there. Anyway, I was hardly one to talk. I've buried my share of booty and plum forgotten where the lot of it was. We're no better than bloomin' squirrels, pirates.
Tells me he can't shake the feeling it's buried in the Lost Boys' hideout. The House Under the Tree.

I tell him it can't be.
Safest place from a pirate in all of Neverland, says he.
No one remembered why pirates never set foot in the Lost Boys' hideout in the hollow of that tree. It was nothing doing. No matter that them runts were armed with naught but slingshots and toy swords. Took a buccaneer with more salt than any on the Jolly Roger to swagger within spitting distance of that gnarled old thing. That timber gives us the shivers.
Only hang on, how'd you get in to bury it there in the first place? Queries I.
I must have been quite clever.
You? I've met you. You're not clever.
Maybe I used to be, he says.
So he ventured in, cutlass trembling in hand... and I never saw ol' Barmy again. For all I know he's in there still. Flayed out like some human version of one of them bear rugs.
Though... never mind. It's nothing. It's just that last time we had a run-in with a gang of them urchins, I nabbed one of them by the ankle just as the little blighter was taking flight. I swear he had Norbert's jacket. And he had Norbert's durag. And what's more, he had Norbert's freckles. Now answer me that–how'd them Lost Boys steal the freckles right off Norbert's face? Spitting image of Norbert he was. Only pint-sized, you understand.
At the risk of sounding barmy myself, I say that House Under the Tree did something to Norb. All them games them boys play, right? Storytelling. Make believing. Lazing about doing nothing productive. Why, it makes me green with sick to think on.
Leastaways I hope ol' Barmy laid eyes on his treasure one last time. Some things are best forgotten, says I.
Fetch me another rum, would you. Mine's empty.

Erica Gibson

I painted this calm, wise face on the trunk of a beautiful old cedar, using natural earth pigments and water—materials the tree would recognize. I wanted to honor and respect the tree by using materials found in nature.

Spending time creating something so temporary was really good for my soul. It helped me let go of expectations and just be present with what I was doing. As I worked, I felt like I got to know the tree on a deeper level, like I was connecting with something living and aware inside it.

There was something freeing about making art that might only last a short while. It didn't need to be preserved to matter. Just being there in that moment, creating with care and intention, was enough.

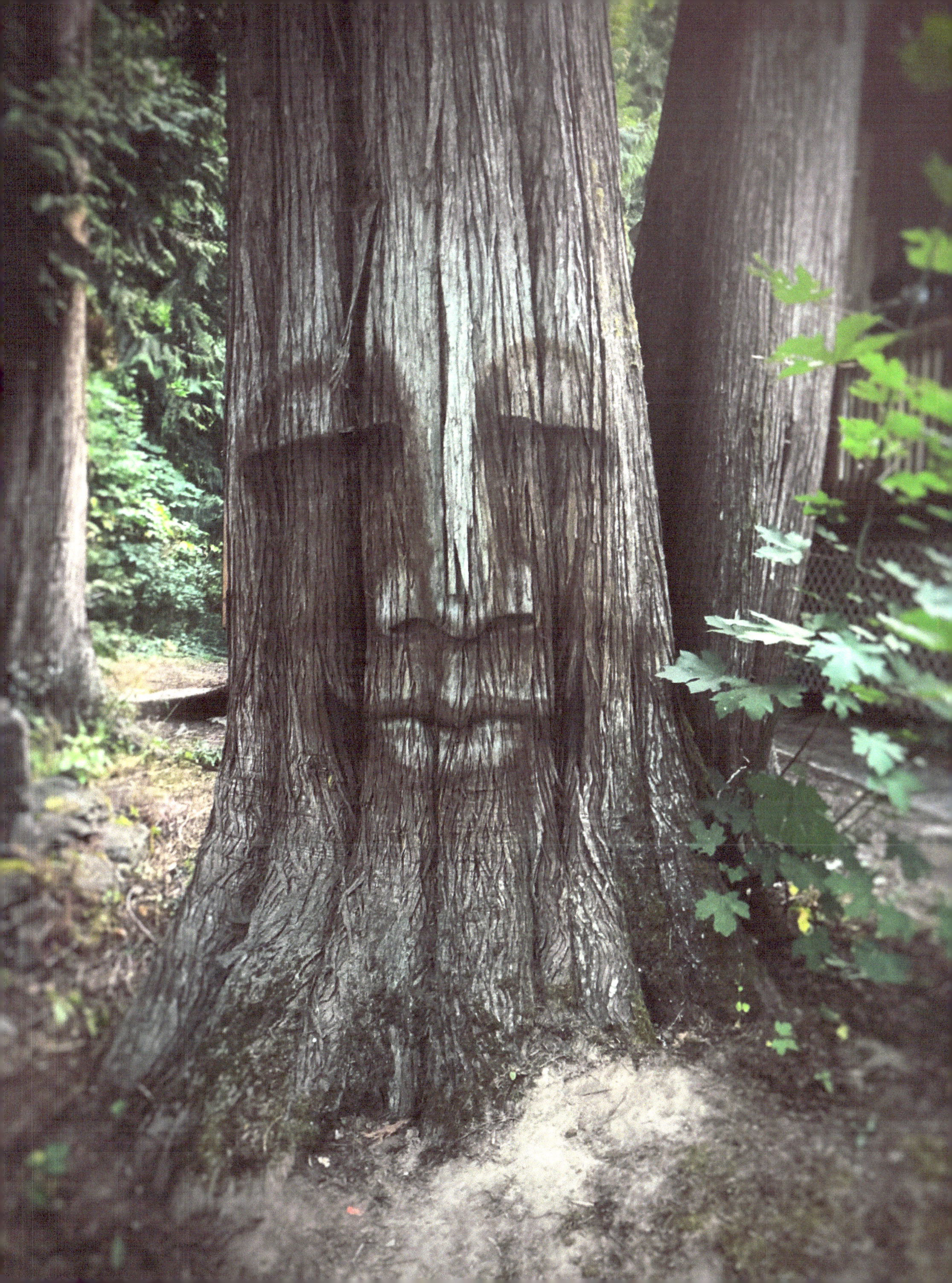

Merridawn Duckler

On Making and Unmaking

First an idea comes to you that is so wide you have to drive around it for a while.
At the same time it is as small as any chance of survival.
You think: ideas come in all seasons we owe them nothing. But this idea is like the spider web you blunder through walking on the trail.
Clingy.
Like a little piece of string that keeps riding shotgun on your jacket even after you've flicked it away.
So you accept that the idea is staying.
You can't return it anyway because you don't know where it came from.
The idea has lowtack pressure sensitive adhesive; it has stickiness and persistence
That is how you know it is good.
You look for a vessel for your idea, to contain and protect it.
It is spring.
The idea is running around, exploring the world, putting out tendrils, getting in the trouble of the innocent.
You're absorbed in the lifestyle of your idea. Everything is new and experimental.
The idea is a shapeshifter but rife with passions. You settle into a rhythm. You might try to anticipate
but there are surprises.
The idea is gaining strength and time races along.
The idea is contoured, shapely, muscular, sexy, exceptional and quotidian.
It is summer.
The container for your idea is part of it now.

The days lengthen and idea's shimmer across the fields. The nights cool only for stars.
You give freedoms to your idea. It's roots are deep and strong.
It's in rhythm with all the world around it.
Lazily self-sufficient.
Then one day, just like any other, the idea shivers. A little cold valley begins to run through it.
Nice and cool.
You watch the idea loosen its ties to the sustaining trunk.
The idea is not losing potency so much as falling into fugue.
It turns from green and flaxen to russet and vermillion.
Shorter now, the light.
It is fall.
The core values in the idea deepen. The wind picks them up and tosses them.
Parts of the idea have departed, seeking warmth.
Sections shed. The idea tries on beauty's cosplay like a peacock.
The idea is no longer giving away seeds but hugging them to itself.
In the once dusty ground a husk forms around the idea hard as a diamond brooch.
The idea no longer shifts but stays very still.
It is winter.
Snow falls, making the outlines of the idea perfectly visible.
The air is sharp around the idea. There's glass between the fire and it's outage.
Something that was always in it is silent.
The idea is blinding with a sharp inward gasp.
You hold the container.
There is a version of love between you and the idea.
You took it and it unmade you. Flaws and disappointment, wrong turns and dustbins. Majesty. Regret. It wasn't quite what you thought. It was everything you had to have.
You get in your car and drive around.
You put your hand out the window.
Move.

Jim Stewart

The Mossararium was created during my residency at Verdancy in May of 2022, using various species of moss and other items, including rocks from a rock pile (now the rock library) and some rusty metal. It was one of a series of projects where I was exploring the possibilities of using living creatures to create art.

Mosses are non-vascular plants, meaning that they have no root system. They absorb water directly through their tiny leaves. When ambient water is not available, they go into cryptobiosis, a state of suspended animation, from which they revive during wetter conditions.

Mosses are host to a number remarkable animals that can also go into cryptobiosis in response to dry or freezing conditions. Nematodes are tiny, ubiquitous worms that feed on bacteria and are in turn subject to predation by carnivorous fungi. Bdelloid rotifers, also found in this mossarium, are microscopic filter feeders that use a wheel of cilia to draw in water. The are all female. Both species have been revived after being frozen in Siberian permafrost for tens of thousands of years.

Mosses are host to tardigrades, which are also known as moss bears. Tardigrades are microscopic eight-legged creatures that are notoriously indestructible when dehydrated into their cryptobiotic state. Some have survived the vacuum and cosmic radiation of space.

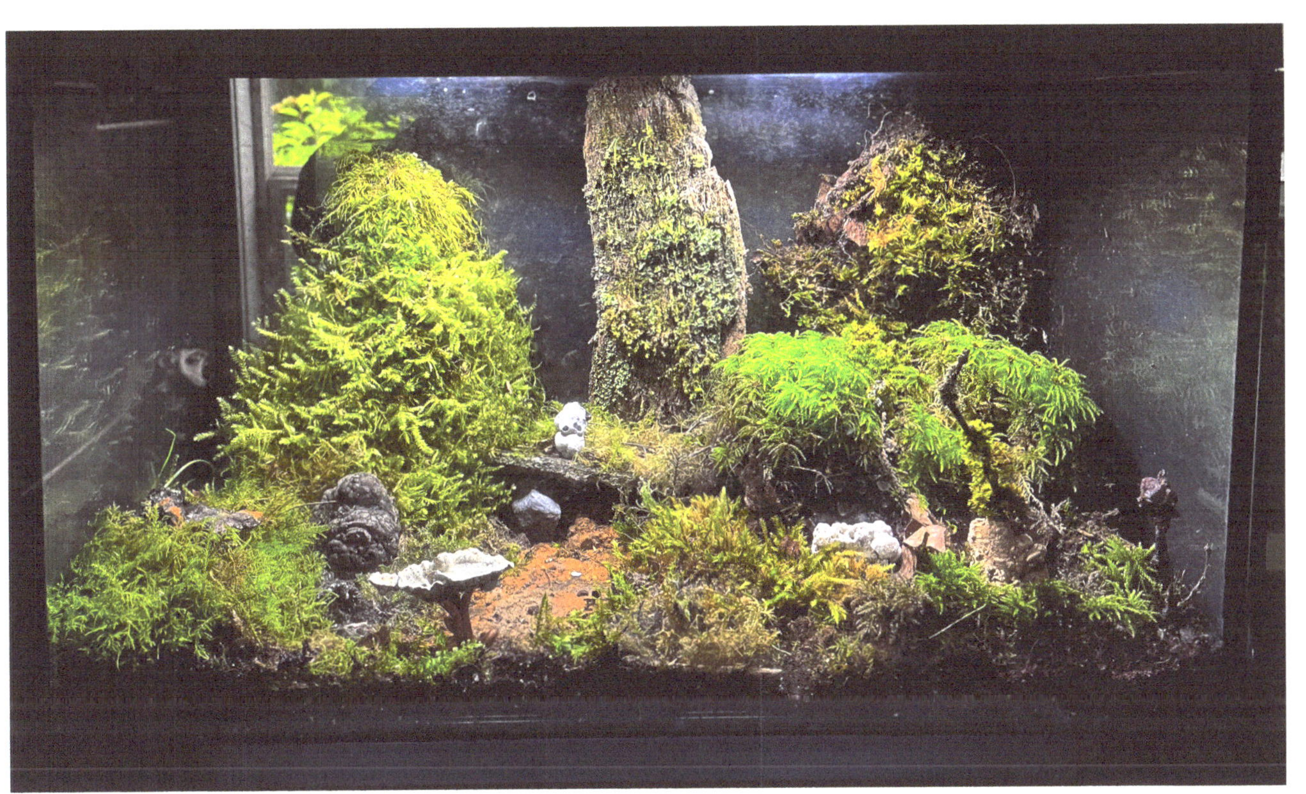

Juliet Johnson

I arrived with little beyond a mental image of my body curled into the earth. I had been ruminating about the forest floor as a space rich with life & death cycles–bubbling & cacophonous–and the way disabled bodies live in intimacy with death. So I brought gifts and made a space where I felt welcomed. It became a daily ritual: under the redcedar, as close as I could get to the humus, resting towards belonging, like a changeling laid in the snow to be taken back to the fae, I slept.

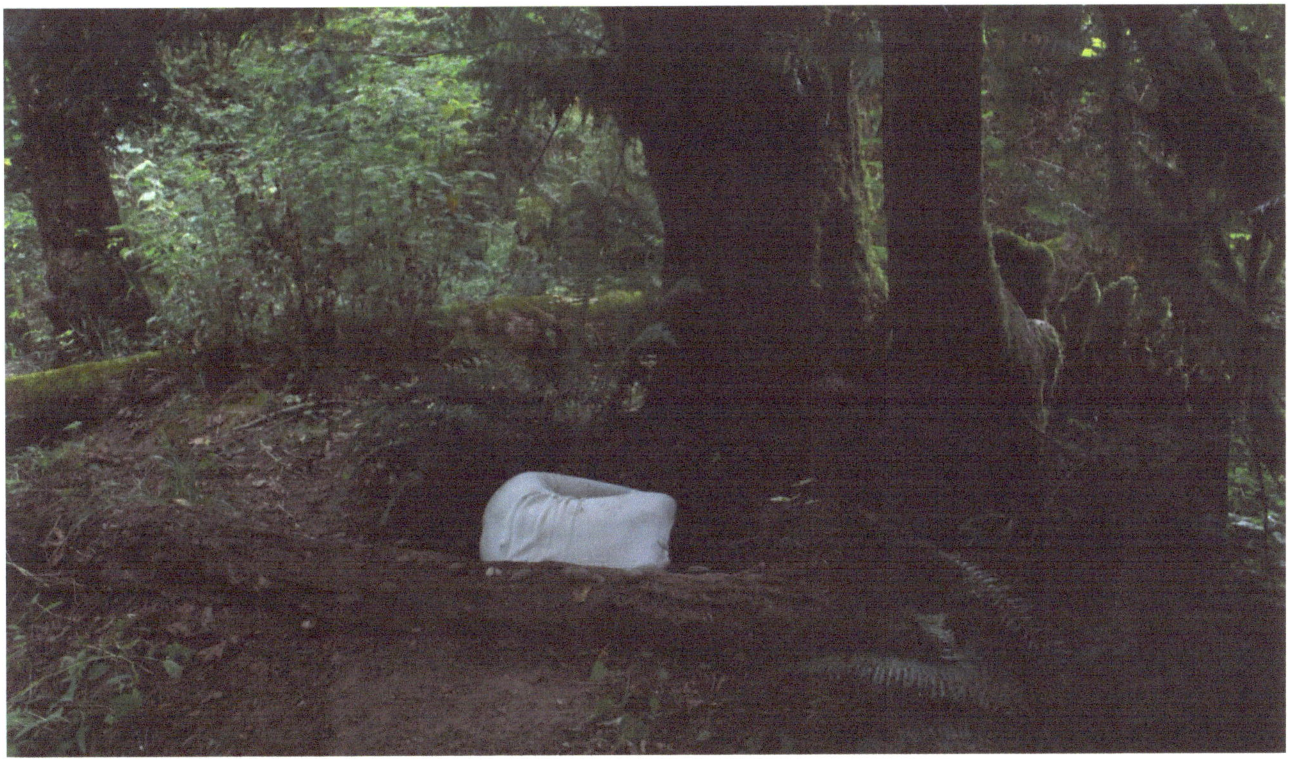

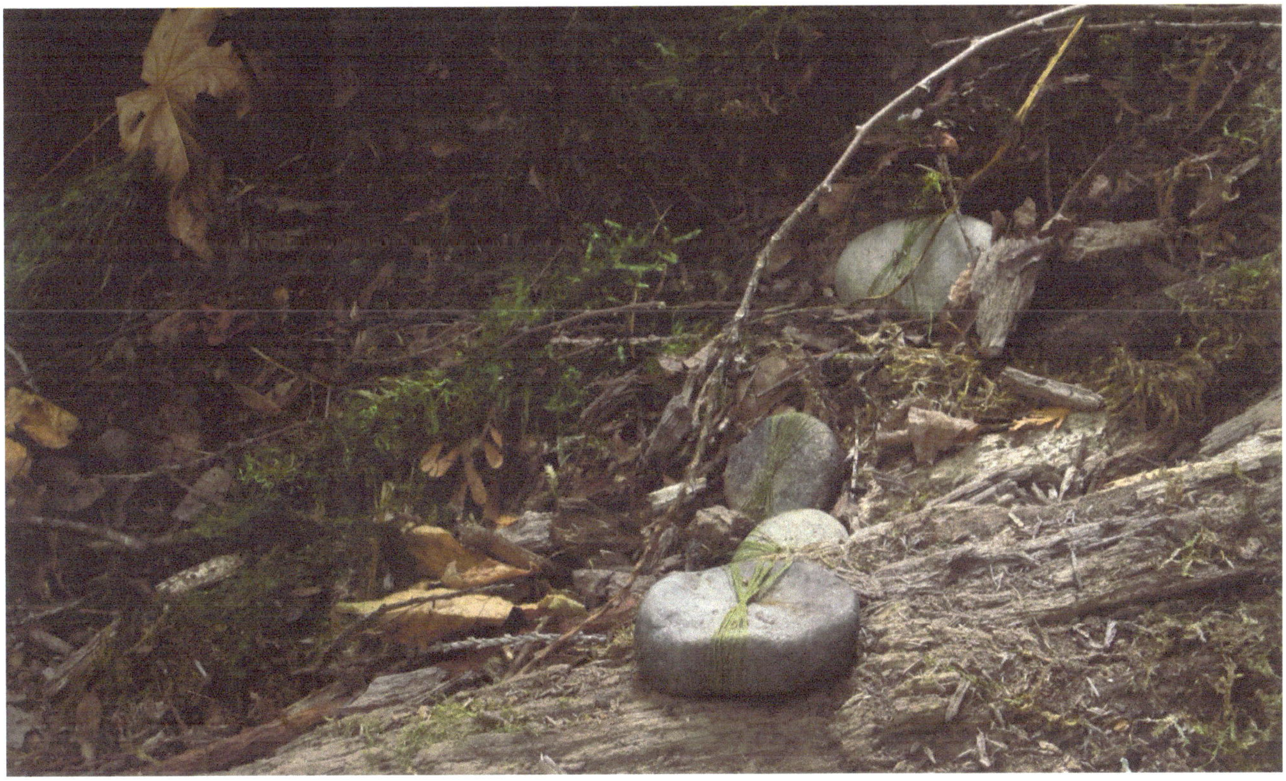

Corey S. Pressman

An Eschatology

Speed this swamp,
stop-motion fast-forward
generations of sun, moon,

and stars reflect less
and less, as the
sky receives the bracken,

cattails sway and succumb,
make way for some
future forest where we

lay in the slow shade
pulling soft days
out of the hard ground.

The Audacity

It was a half
century of tossed
terrain, false alarms,
invisible enemies

before I would
attempt something
that reflects
remotely the echoing
abstract air of this place.
But for
the audacity of the
sand dollar—
specimen of imperfect
elegance, even
when crushed by
a black tire, breaks beautifully

in the tracks.
But for
the way an underwave slips
and sizzles up-sand and,

at its apex,
deposits delicate

scraps: small
wood, kelp confetti,

tiny dots
of white shell,
as if to say:

After all these miles
of midnight,
fathoms of drowned
and ciliated brilliance,
by this glinting scrim,
by my tender old
lullaby:

I found these
for you.

Leiana Petlewski

My time at the Verdancy Project allowed me to truly experience the cycles of nature. For the first time in a long time, I allowed myself to rest, unfold the layers, and breathe. This allowed the seeds of new ideas and inspiration to take root and have room to grow at their own rate, rather than feeling the need to produce as much as possible as fast as possible.

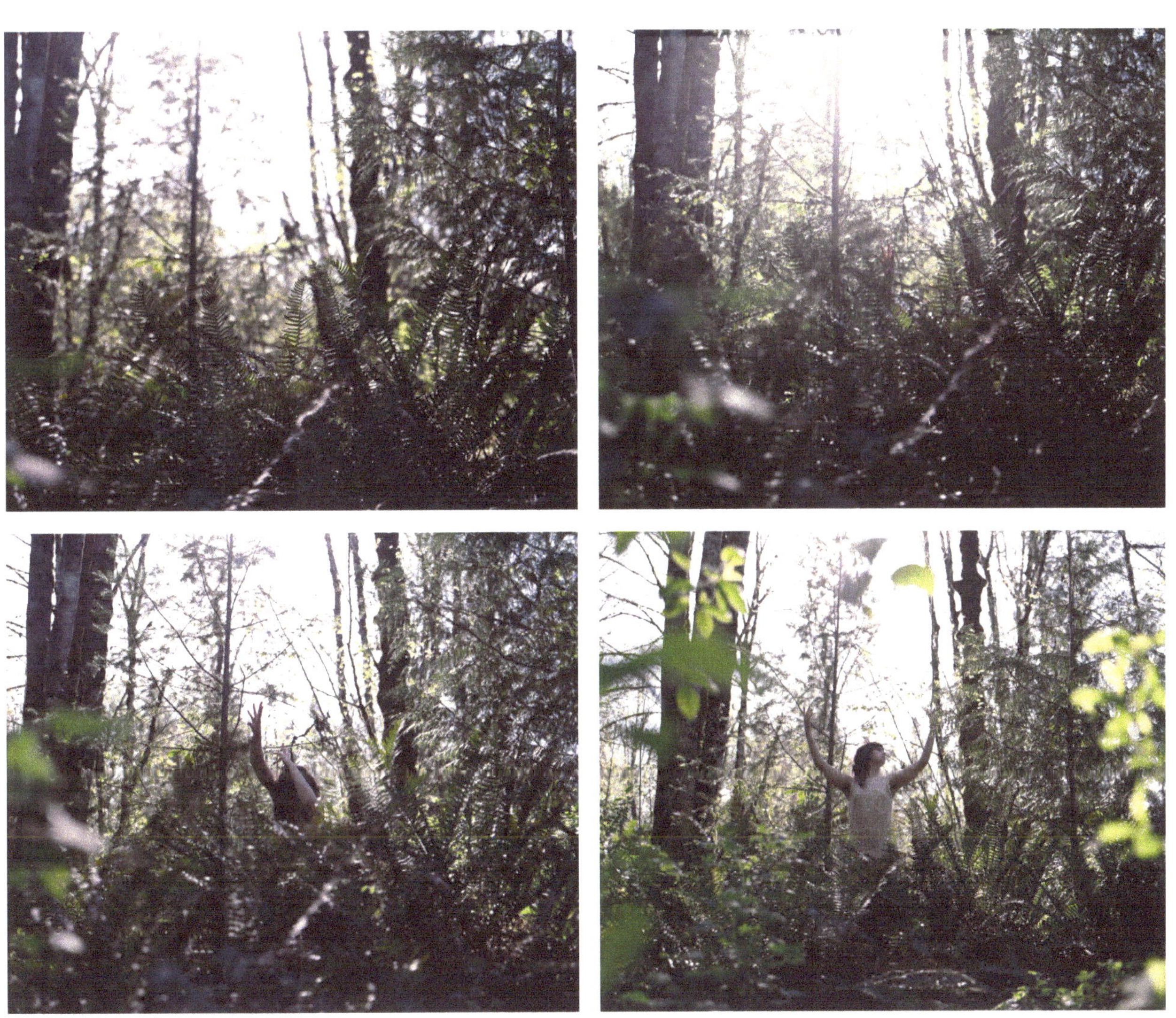

A reflection and exploration of what it is to unfold, stretch, and grow both in the micro sense, like a fern, and in the macro sense, like the seasons and cycles of the year.

Morgan Barnett

During my time at The Verdancy Project, I became interested in synchronous shapes, gentle methodical rituals, and sculpting into river clay. I spent nights in the tree house listening to raccoons splash in the river, which became a collaboration as I placed clay mounds for them to interact with, as if they were bits of treasure to uncover. This shaped the work I would make a few years later by re-learning clay and thinking about water carving river banks and tumbling rocks through time, and how indentations in mud and soil are the result of interactions between flora, fauna and elements that create form through function. I have been exploring the idea of vessels for epiphytes that would be both usable planters that suit the needs of the plant while also maintaining organic sculptural design.

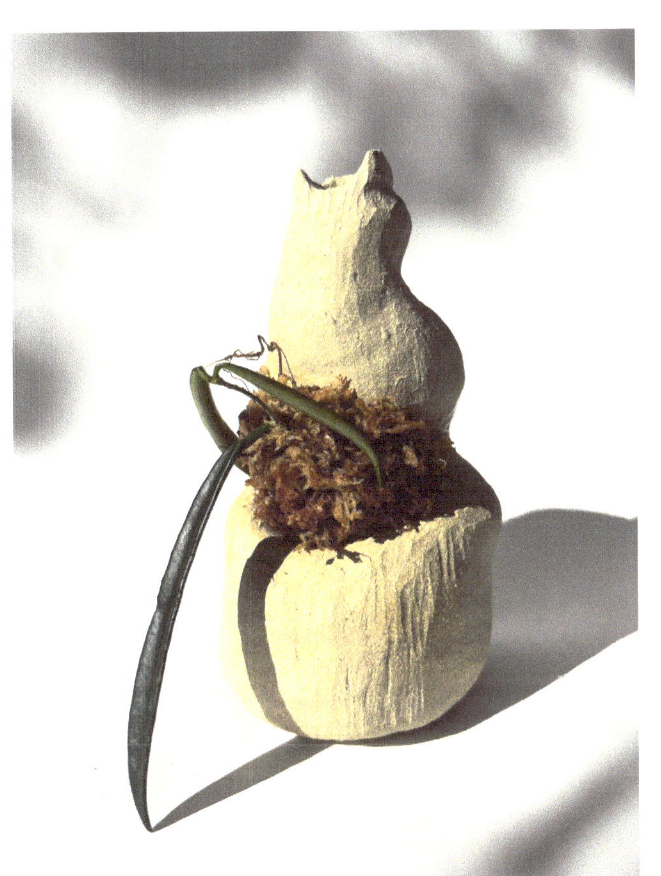

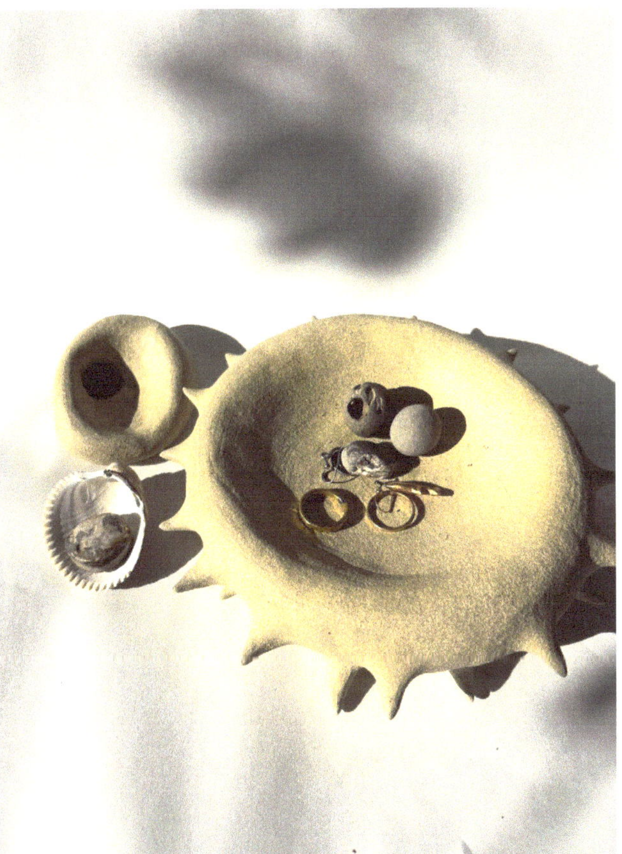

Shelly Smith

This postcard-sized work depicts some of the diatoms, desmids, and other microbial forms I observed in water samples collected on the residency grounds.

My artwork explores the microbiome as an identifier of place, as each microbiome makes a specific environment unique. During my residency at The Verdancy Project, I explored the larger microbiome of where the Columbia River met the Willamette River, including the Sandy River, the snowmelt of Mt. Hood, and water sources around the project grounds. Looking at these samples under the microscope helped ground me in the microbiome of the residency, exploring a new microscopic world.

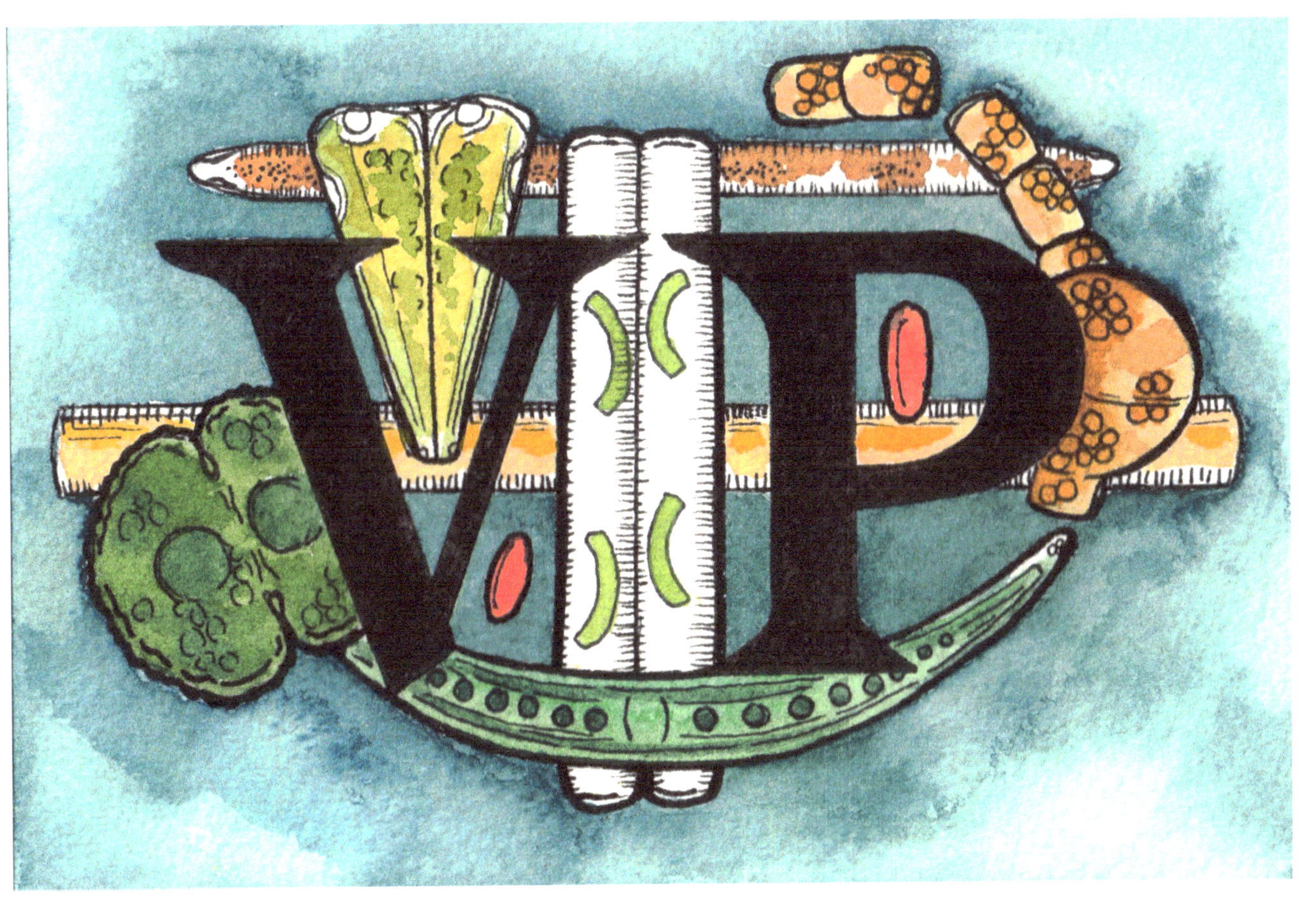

The Verdancy Project is surrounded by agricultural land. This started my chain of thinking of how, through plant starts, nursery trees, and foodways, the microbiome of the Columbia-River area is transported all over the country and beyond. I still think a lot about how the microbiome of the TVP has been transplanted to many locations, its unique bacterial and microbial life finding new homes in gardens and stomachs. I am lucky enough to have observed a snapshot of that under the microscope.

Magda Permut

When I embarked on my residency at The Verdancy Project, I did not know what to expect. I had been engaged in several earth-focused land projects and thought that one of them would step forward once I set aside the protected time to practice. But as I arrived and settled into the sweet cabin, the sound of the creek gurgling and lulling, the setting sun winking at me through the trees, I found a sense of nostalgia coming over me. As I settled into that sweet, sad, longing feeling, I realized I had been writing for years now without reviewing my work or synthesizing it for publication. My time at TVP became about laying in the fields reading my old journals, staring up at the sky or through the dandelion fronds. It became about leaning out the window of the treehouse asking questions about what was needed now from this work, and what was next for me. This small piece, remembering my time in Baltimore and connecting it to the little snail shells that grace the sandy riverbanks, became the first answer to these ponderings. If I could, I would place it like a smooth stone someplace on the TVP property for you to happen across. I wish it would shine back your own reflection if you find it wet with rain.

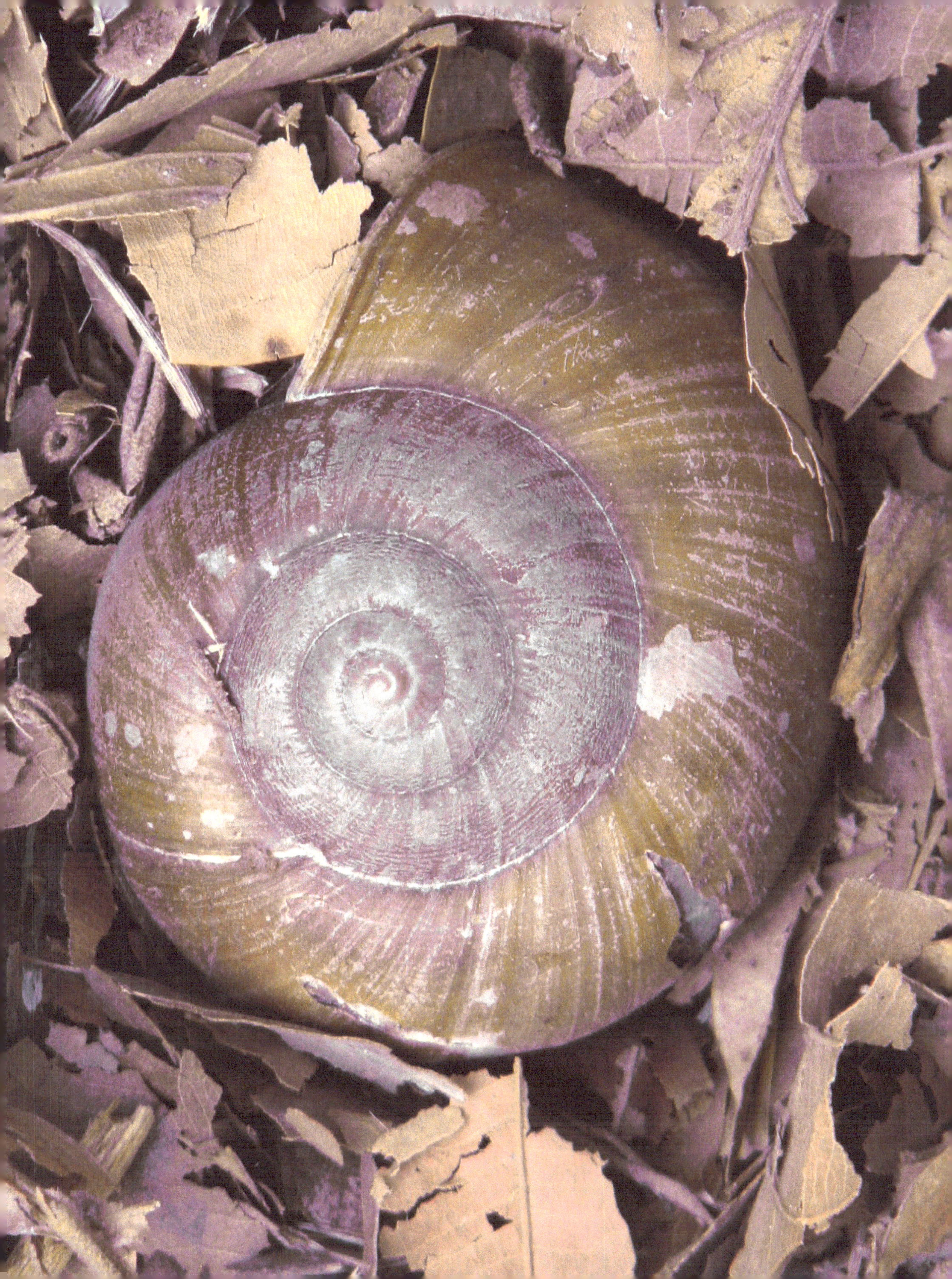

Magda Permut

Spiral

In the National Aquarium in Baltimore there is a tank that has a spiral ramp in the middle. The tank is all around this ramp, and with each turn of the descent, the hardscape of coral reefs, sea plants, seaweed, and the stationary softscape of anemones, starfish, and cave dwelling eels change. The sharks, grouper, and porcupinefish all circle at different speeds and in different directions. And as I descend, I feel like a part of a grand process, one that I have only a small amount of agency over but that has a rhythm and pace to it—an interconnection. Other people in the aquarium also circle down or up the ramp at different paces; they too are of different shapes and sizes. We all move around and around and around.

When I return to any particular point in the spiral, I see familiar landscape—a giant rock or a log. A notable crustacean. At first, my brain registers the familiarity —I know this place! But then, when I have a moment to sit with it, I realize it is not exactly the same. I am at a different height, the angle is different. And so, although that stone was there before and I know it, I can now see its shiny underbelly and the algae growing there. And the fish that met me at eye level at the previous loop are now slightly above, and I see their lighter bellies, smooth and taut rather than their stripe-finned sides.

The soul journey is like this. We like to think that progress is a straight line but that is a falsehood of the materialist mind. The journey sometimes feels like a circle (and often the ways we try to do the journey without wise support can be a circle, following our blind spots round and round). But if we have a sincere desire to grow and change, and we have wise support, the journey is more of a spiral. There is a deepening. It is circular, but in three dimensions. Like the seasons. Every year there is a spring, but it isn't the same Spring.

Sometimes the darkness is overwhelming. If we have done some unproductive circling before we truly get on our soul journey, we are sensitized to fear getting stuck in a loop. And so we see the things that look the same, that recurring part of the spiral, and we panic. The fear brain screams: I am here again! Look—it's THAT rock! That same fucking speckled rock! I am not going anywhere. I am going in circles. This isn't working. There is no journey. Just my same dumb loop.

And this is the point where I ask us to pause, to stay with the familiar long enough to look at it more closely. If you do this, you can see that you are in the same spiral, but it is not exactly the same because you are at a different angle. That rock is still that rock. (Of course it is that rock—it's YOUR journey! That is YOUR ROCK! You may see that rock for the rest of your days as it is your karma in some way—you and that rock are intimately linked in ways understandable and not.) But you are different—you are seeing that rock from a different angle.

Contextualizing our journey this way can help us adjust to the rhythm of the soul life. It is not a line, but that does not mean that it does not follow a pattern. It is just a pattern more ancient and rhythmic than the rise-over-run of modern productivity. As we descend into ourselves, our presence deepens and so the energy gets more dense, more intense. We become more the naturally sensitive being we were always meant to be and so become less tolerant of things that do not suit our soul life. We learn to build a kind of sea legs, a metabolism that allows us to withstand the pressures of the depths and to trust the inner path's unfolding. And we gradually also become acclimated to the truth that each of us is a part of a dynamic and intricate ecosystem whose journey of healing and growth is intricately connected to the journey of every other thing.

Because unlike the Baltimore aquarium, our depths don't end. They just keep going, keep circling, keep richening. The soul journey has unfathomable depths.

Sharon Servilio

Living with the rhythms of the environment, I was able to observe life on different temporal and spatial scales than those accessible in typical human-centric routines. For instance, there was a large sunflower in the garden, and each day new florets opened in concentric spirals from edge to center, and each day the bees fastidiously worked their way toward the center pollinating the tiny blooms. This flower held a portal to an entire universe of other ways of being, and inspired several sculpture ideas.

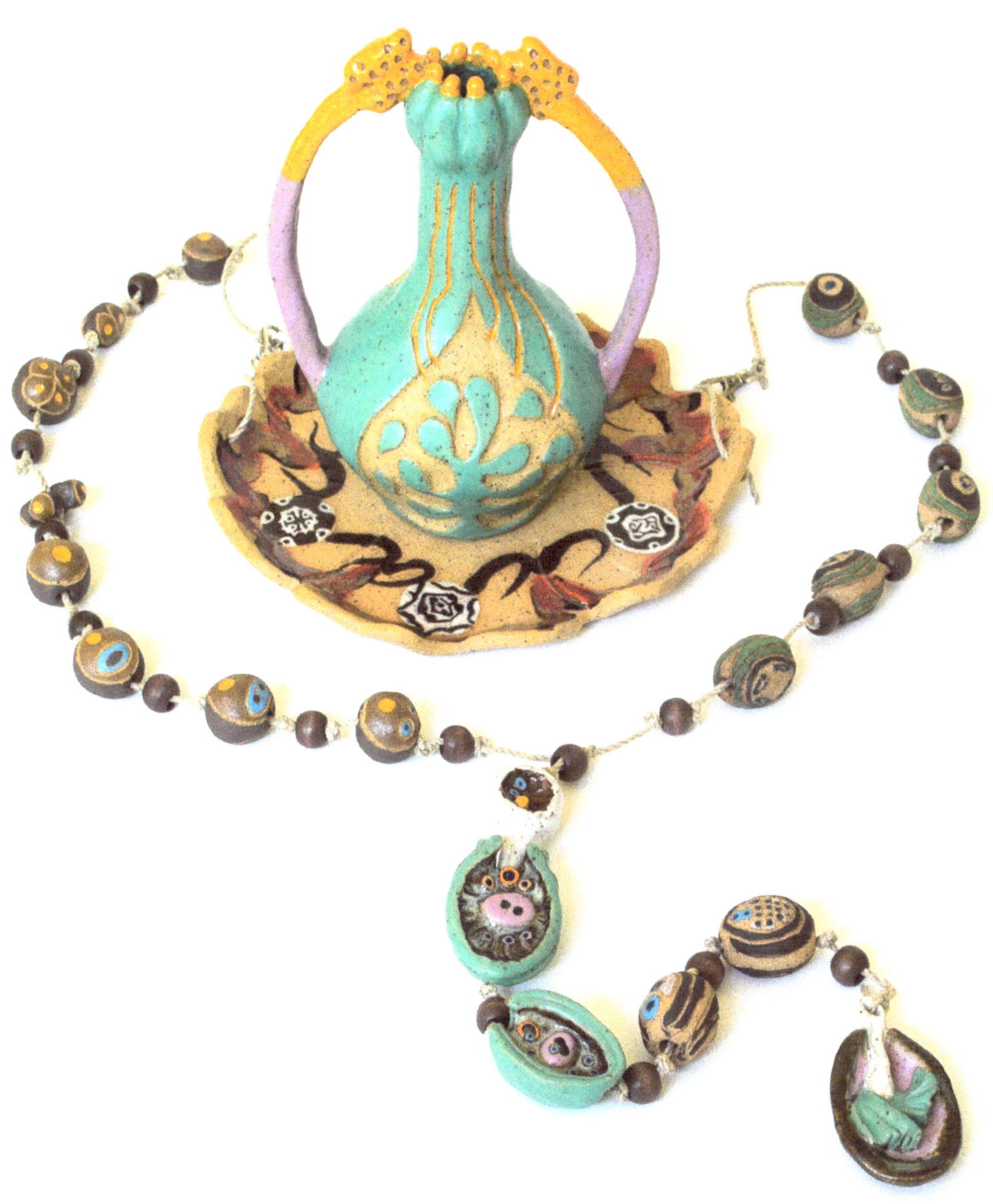

Amy Ash

What can we learn from the kinship of tangled roots and whispering rhizomes, the sharing of resources for mutual flourishing, and the vibrant reemergence after a long winter of rest?

My interdisciplinary practice is deeply invested in methodologies of collective care. This has led me to pursue sustainable, slow, and intentional methods of making objects that care for both human and more-than-human bodies. Natural rhythms, sensorial play, and methodologies of care feature across my interdisciplinary practice.

I'm interested in broadcasting a gentle reminder of the wisdom to be learned from multi-species community and a call to honour the ecosystems we belong to with our attention and care. In doing so, perhaps we can better support those we are in community with and begin to fully embrace our own cycles of resilience, from seeding, growth, and flourishing, to loss, rest, and, particularly, regrowth.

The Verdancy Project gave me invaluable time and space to explore, play, and sink into the present moment. It's a place that embraces slowness and rewards curiosity. The lush environment also echoes through my work in pigments and shadows that coalesce as compositions of natural dye and cyanotype on textile. Every moment was a pleasure.

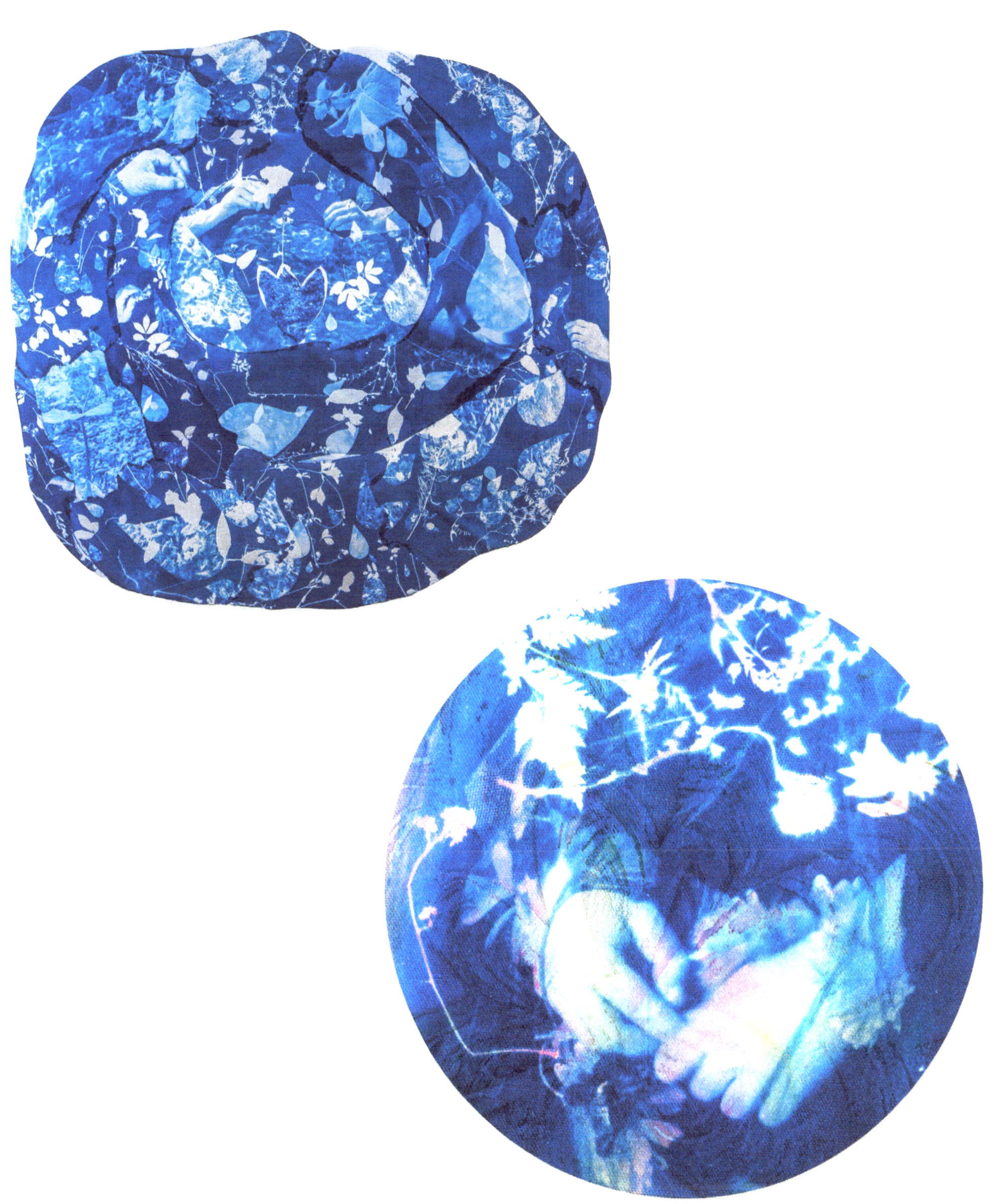

Bedrock Theatre

A sniff of Air. A touch of Water. A taste of Earth. A sound of Fire.

In a clearing ringed by tall Cedars, the Nature Bar beckons. Elemental flavors, with pairings of story and song, await the traveler who dares to step off the path, pause and sip from their surroundings.

The Nature Bar, Bedrock's immersive installation and performance, focused on the four elements—Earth, Water, Fire and Air—characterizing these components of The Verdancy Project landscape through song, movement, storytelling and sensory offerings. Passing audience members stepped off the path to order from an elemental menu, and received a short performance just for them. The Nature Bar drew attention to the decadent sensory feast around us at all times, and demonstrated our innate ability to connect with our environment as beings who evolved in tandem with all we experience in the natural world.

The Nature Bar was Bedrock's first performance after four years of Pandemic hiatus. We were a little rusty, getting back into it—we doubted our ideas, struggled to commit to our choices, battled the realities of outdoor producing in summer (heatwaves, wildfire smoke). The Nature Bar finally clicked into place when we allowed ourselves to become quiet and present within the landscape and with each other. Rather than trying to do, do, do and solve the "problem" of the piece, we paused in the clearing and looked at all the richness available to us right there: tall cedar trees, abundant ferns, shade, a picnic table, dandelions, stones. Out of this quiet place of presence and noticing, lots of things became possible—we found ways to use what was there and to invite our audience into an easy, present, playful engagement with their surroundings (something that's pretty tough to do if you are sweating it out yourself!). We were joyfully surprised by the powerful audience responses to the piece, and felt reinvigorated to engage our company mission afterwards. Our time at TVP was a great gift!

Scan to view a video of the Nature Bar

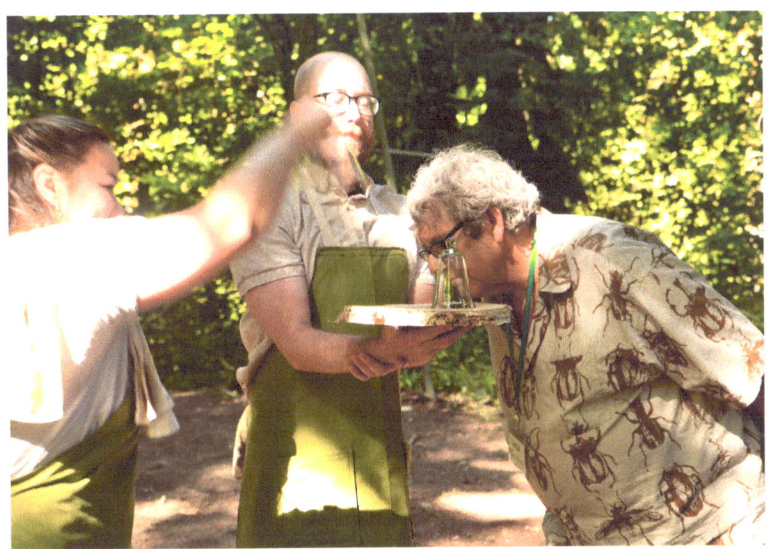

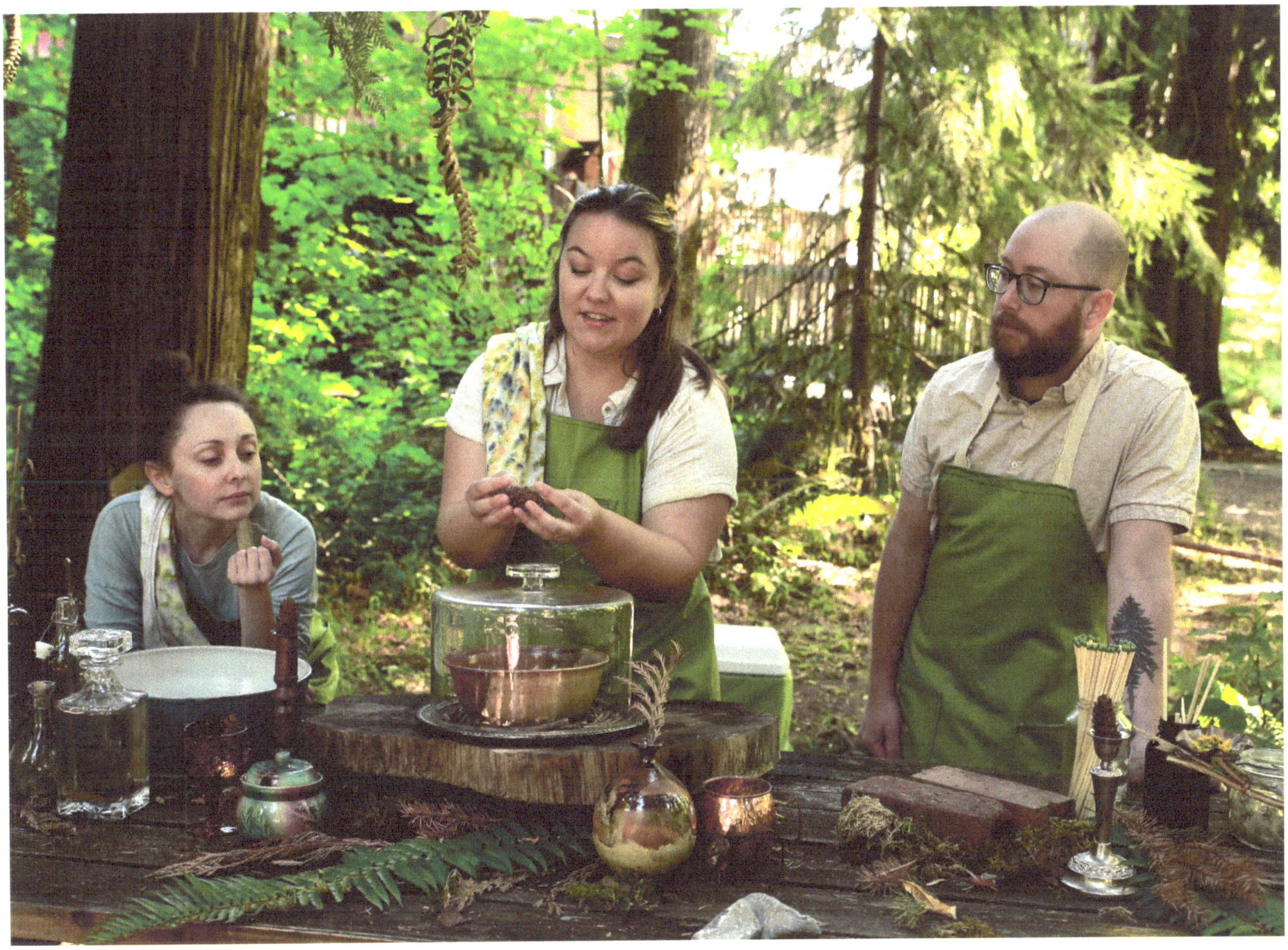

Kendra Larson

This piece incorporates symbols of growth (flowers) and death (skull), as well as the mystery associated with nightscapes—all interests of mine that touch on the cycles of life.

My time at The Verdancy Project's Residency was really a nature-filled feast for my senses; walking through the chilly creek with bare feet, smelling the flowers in the pigment garden, soaking up the heat of the sun at the picnic table, listening to the wind while sketching in the tree house, tasting the raspberries and tomatoes in the garden, and watching the bees working hard in their hive. These rhythms of nature inspired me to take life slower and observe a little more deeply.

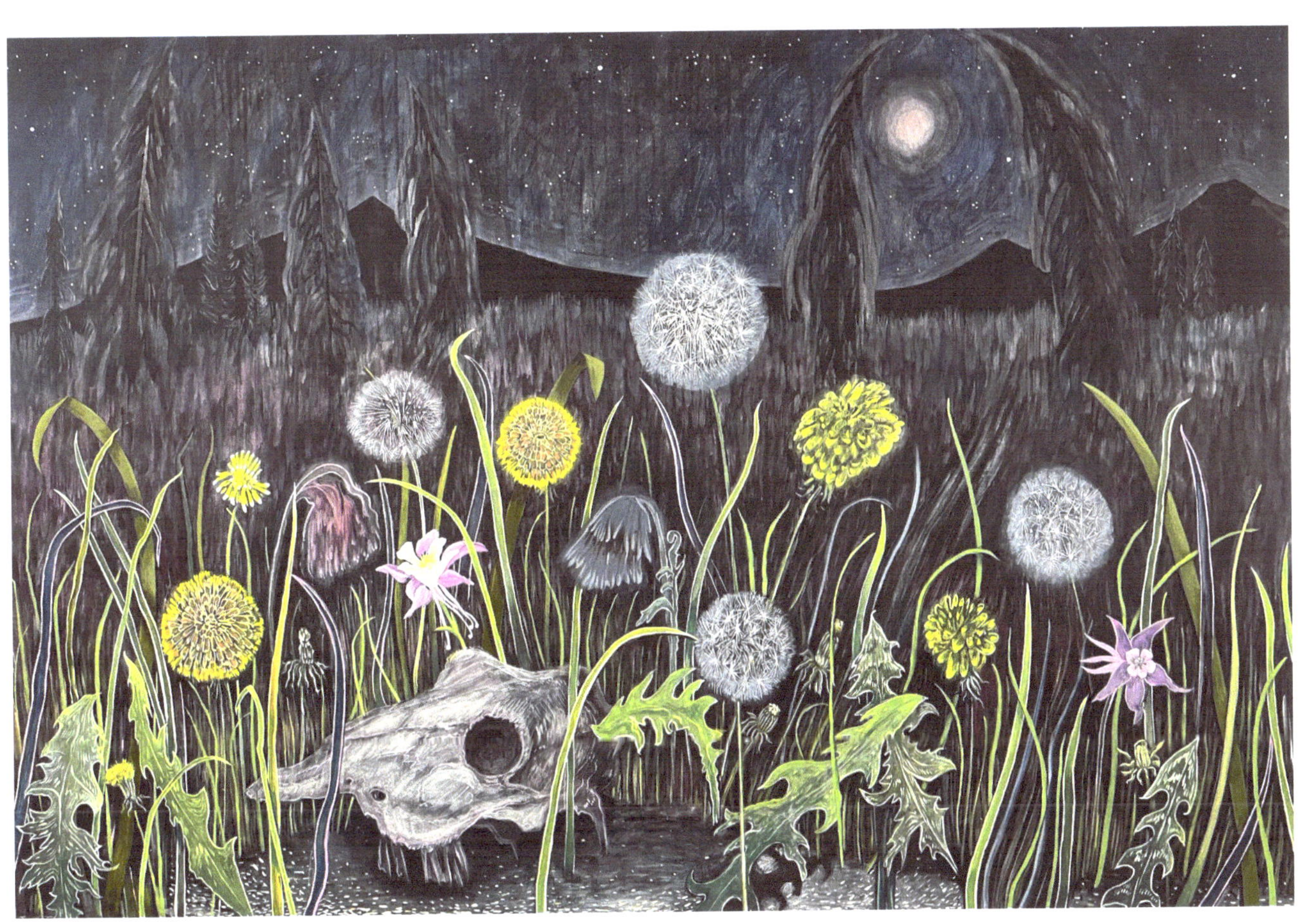

Barb Burwell

These fiber pieces are based on looking at the landscape, noting weather patterns, and witnessing feelings of nostalgia—especially those connected to the idea of place. They are meant to speak to the distilling of a visual language developed to draw and weave connections between these imagined ideas through imagery collected through observation and spending time in various natural settings. I wanted to capture the most basic and elemental shapes, making them the main focus and reducing them to their most potent form.

With this work, I wanted to create new relationships between the lines of thread and the appliquéd fabric forms by layering, blending, and overlapping these shapes, then responding with gestural sewn line work, weaving these marks together with the shapes to create visual connections practically and conceptually.

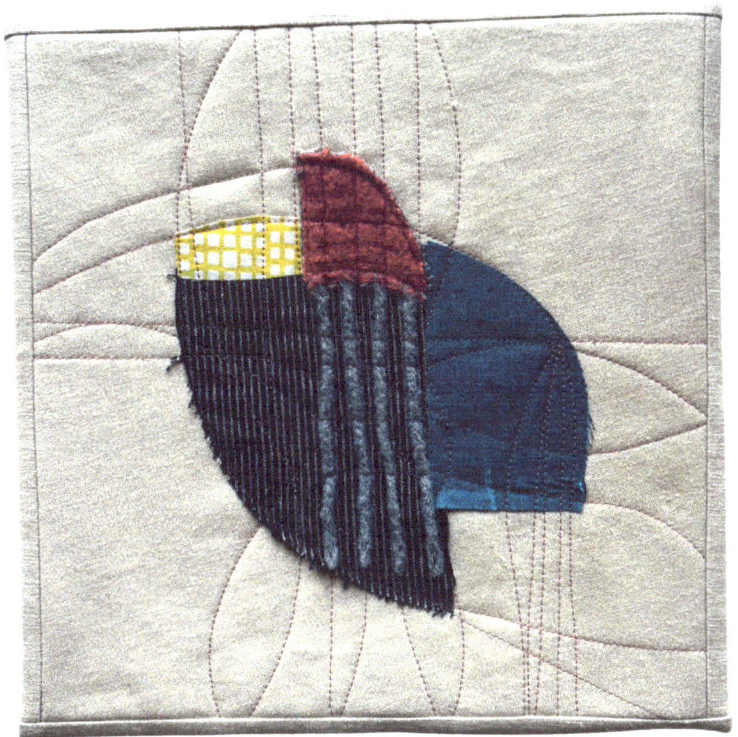

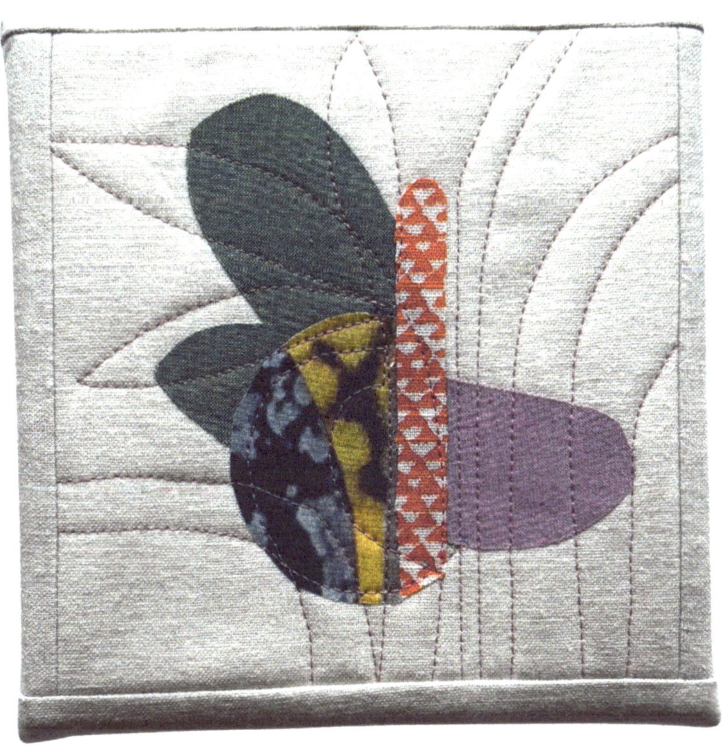

ProLab Dance

Between

Laura Cannon - dancer
Lynne Piper - vocalist
Sculpture by Andy Kennedy

A practice in decomposition. An opportunity for our cells to remember. A meditation on returning the elements we have borrowed.

Between originated as a rehearsal for being dead. Lying in a hole, under the roots of a fir tree, Laura endeavors to let go of her sense of self and dissolve into the forest floor. This piece moves at the speed of decay; incremental shifts accumulate as Laura moves down an embankment to the creek below. Laura's dance is accompanied by Lynne Piper creating live vocal loops that also accumulate incrementally throughout the duration of the piece.

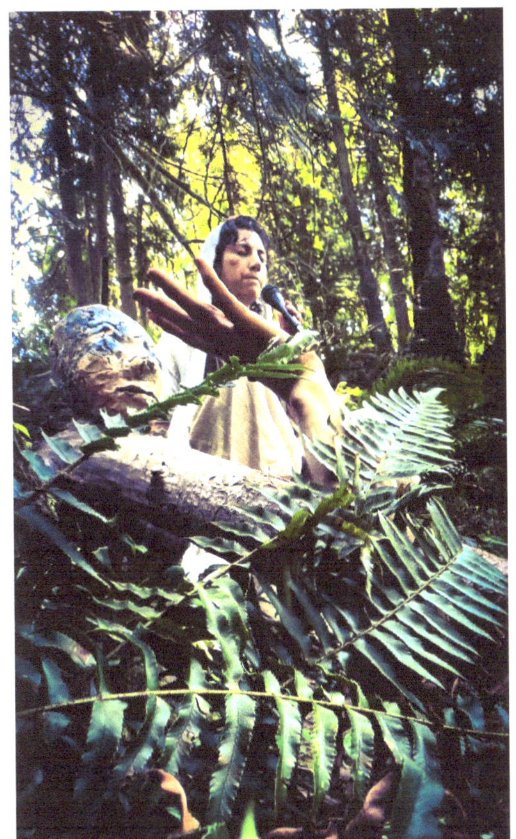

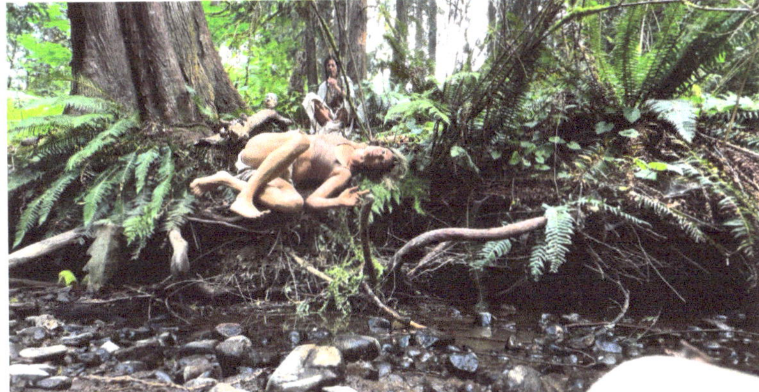

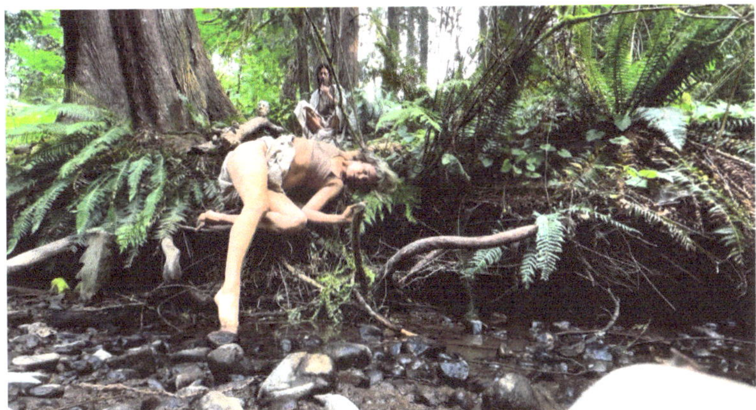

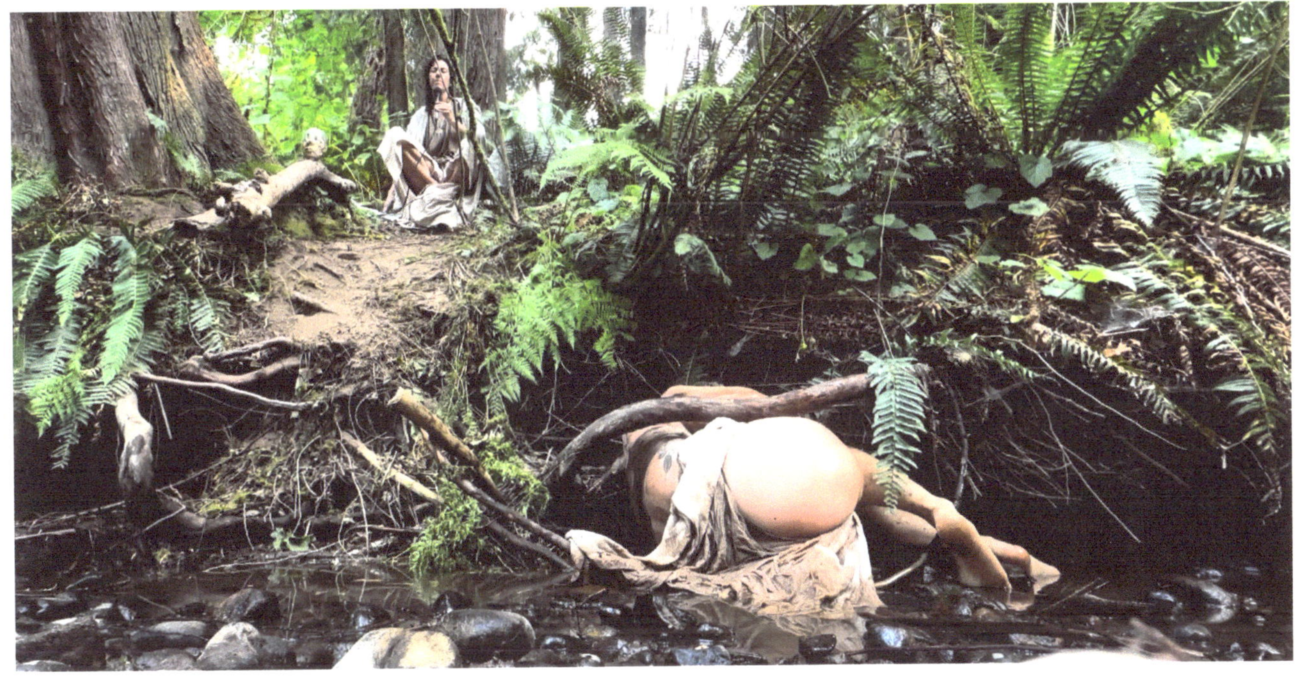

Anne Mavor

These wall pieces are from my earth-friendly and biodegradable series, *Plant Messengers*. For this series, I use botanical contact printing on vintage and reused fabric to create abstracted forms. This work exists as wall pieces and installations that reflect my deepening relationship with the land and process of mending ancestral disconnection. Botanical contact printing as I practice it, is a ritual that starts with listening to the plants. Since all the marks, shapes, and pigments come directly from fresh leaves, stems, and flowers, this collaboration requires me to align my practice with the life cycles of the plants. In response, the prints that come to me reflect the lavish beauty and complexity that grows all around us. I regard plants with awe and gratitude as viewers come to do, too.

For my contribution to Terra Incognita at The Verdancy Project, I created The *Wandering Herbarium*, an interactive plant and art scavenger hunt. It was a magical experience to make friends with the land and the other artists. The learning and relationships keep rippling out into my life.

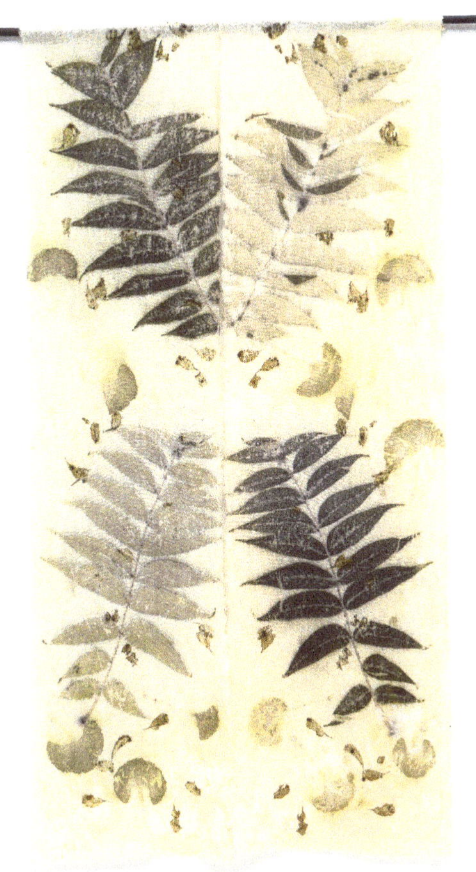

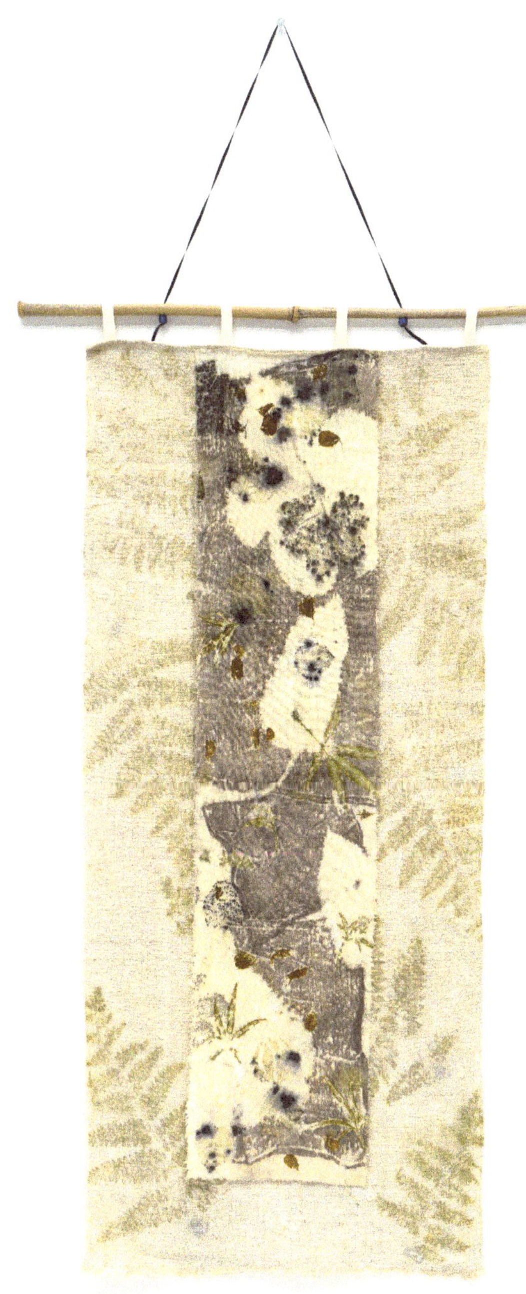

Beth Wilson

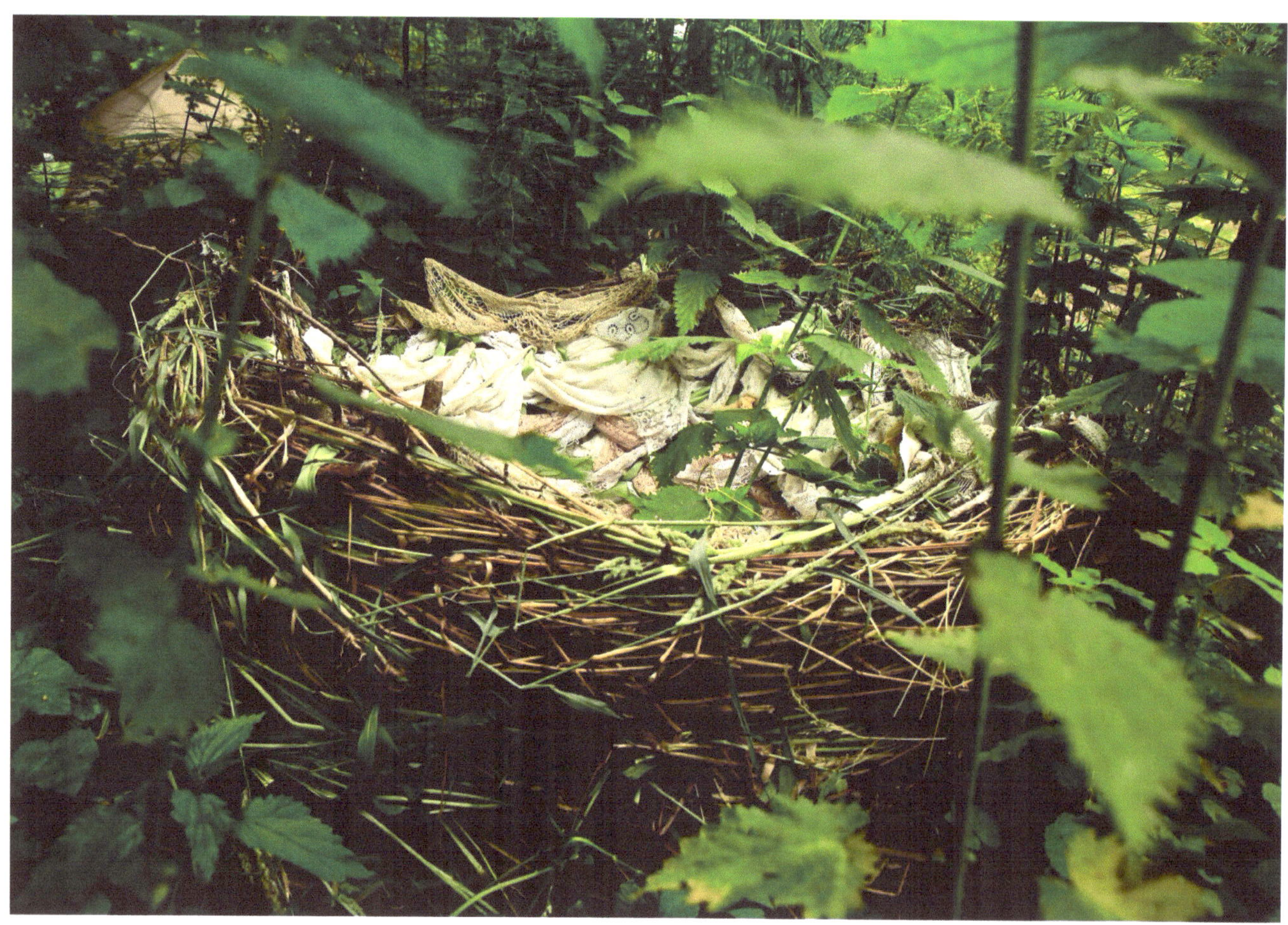

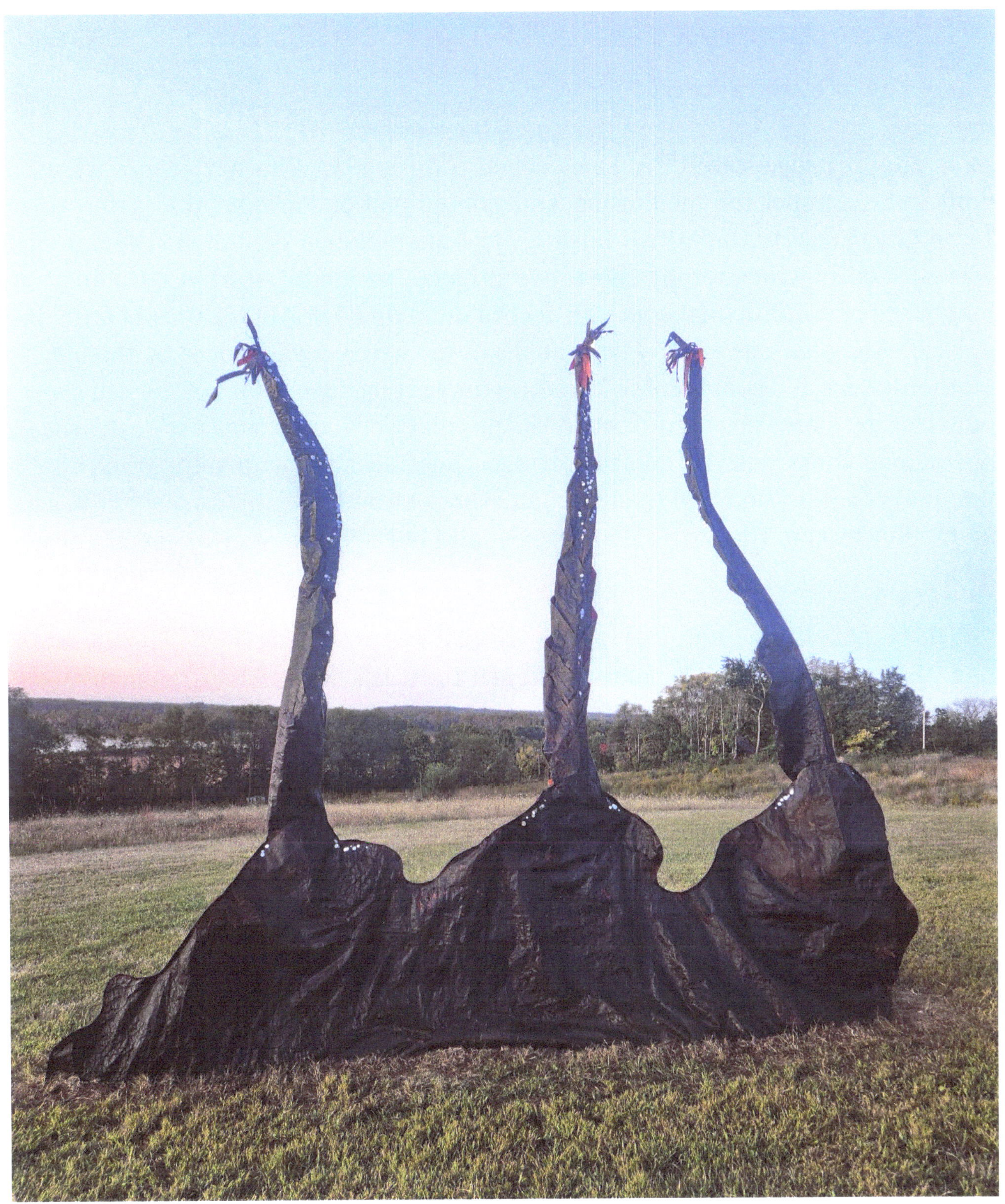

Amber Wolf

I took a class with Olive Loew called "Crafting the Dharma" where we used craft as a channel for meditation and contemplation. Around this same time, I was introduced to the Buried Book Project championed by Emma Freeman and was thrilled how beautifully these two projects melded. I started stitching one long piece of fabric to make into an accordion-style book. Then I started stitching another. The plan was to bury both books in the earth. I was moved by the idea of Mother Nature as a collaborator. I practice mail art partly because of the Zen aspect of it. I let my pieces go out into the world, possibly getting damaged or destroyed by postal machinery, possibly adorning fridges, possibly ending up in the trash after a moment of admiration. I let them go. Sometimes I wonder about the pieces I've sent and if they live on. The Buried Book Project also felt like a wonderful opportunity to let go.

The first book was intuitive. I had no pre-planned idea—I just picked up the fabric and stitched. Then I picked some other fabric to attach and stitched. I thought about this and that as I stitched. The resulting stitches reminded me of a meandering path and that inspired the second book. I thought about the path of life and what one experiences along the way. What kept coming to mind was heartbreak. My brain was distilling life down to a path of heartbreaks and healing. Heartbreak and healing. Heartbreak and healing. If you love, your heart will be broken, time and time again. And, for me, I mended and tended to the broken heart time and time again. This isn't intended to sound gloomy, and I hope you won't see it that way. I believe to live fully, you must go forward with love and an open heart. Inevitably, things you hoped for don't come to pass, loved ones die, irreconcilable differences bring connections to a close, the government fails its people, and your heart breaks because you care and you love. And you grieve and you rest and you go out and love some more. And you grieve and you rest and you go out and love some more. And you grieve and you rest and you go out and love some more.

So I buried both books, one on top of the other, in early July. I shared this experience with a handful of folks, all of us choosing the land of The Verdancy Project for burial. I returned to unearth the books after they had been in the ground for 5 weeks. The results were surprising and stark. The first book, though altered, was largely intact. The heartbreak book, in shambles. So many possible stories and metaphors to draw. Perhaps you can join me in contemplating them.

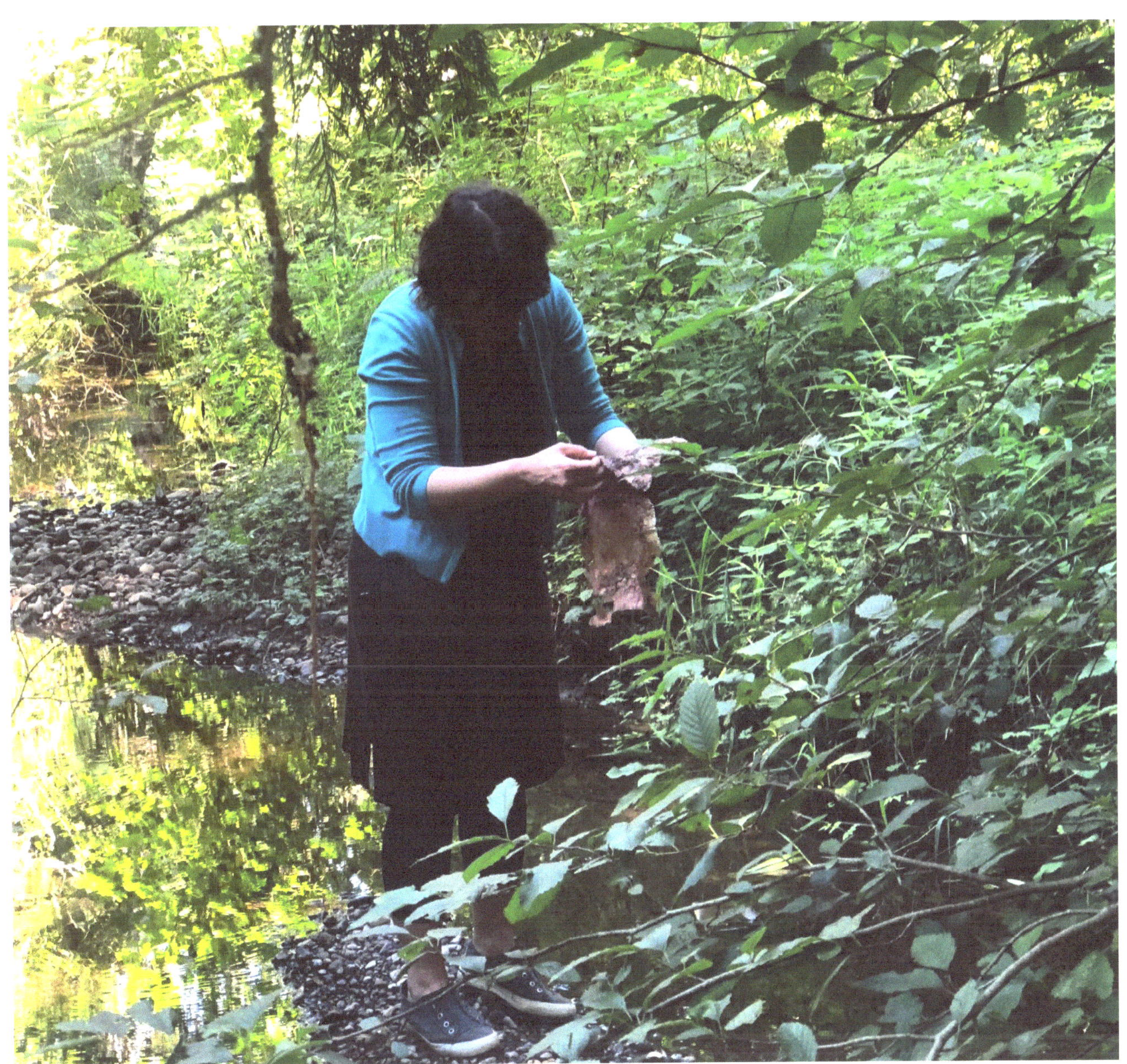

Sami Wax

The woods know what to do with a body gets its title from the short story *Fruiting Bodies* by Kathryn Harlan, which I read while sitting by the creek at TVP. The phrase is multilayered and has contrasting meaning with one interpretation of decay as part of the natural cycles and another with the woods as a healing practice for our bodies. This piece juxtaposes the natural environment with layered text-to-speech audio and a disjointed editing style. The interrupted cycles in the sounds and layered visuals ultimately end up creating a cycle of their own as the flowing water frames my exploration.

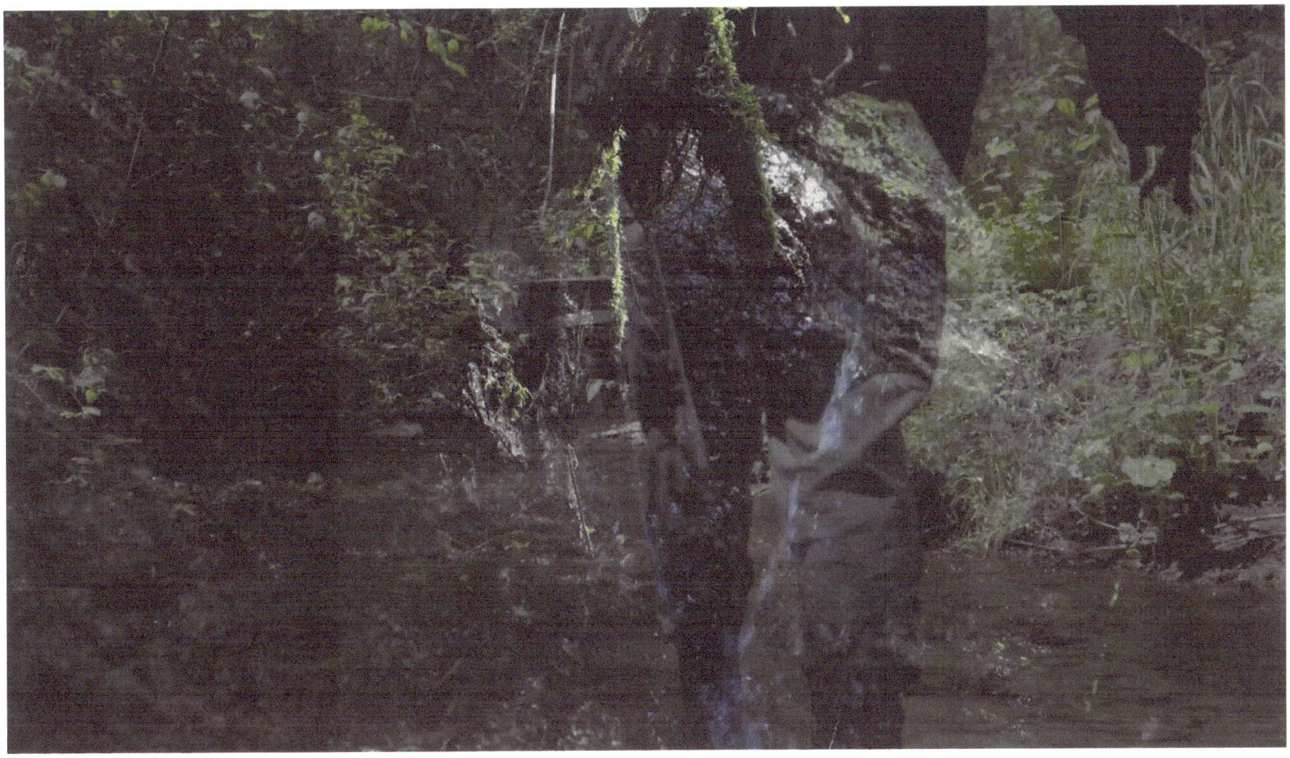

Scan to view video

Sierra Weir

When I visited TVP in 2022, I created in near-solitude for about one month. I was transitioning from Louisiana to Pittsburgh, did not consider myself an artist, and was trying to find my place as someone who had studied the science of pigments. This experience was a critical turning point for me, allowing me the space to connect with myself and the land all while feeling supported by Shannon and other amazing artists in the PNW. From LA to OR I shipped my mortar and pestle, granite slate and pickle weight muller, glass jars, and pigment books in a very heavy box and proceeded to wake up every morning to greet the stream, the rock beach, and the new-to-me ecosystem. I learned about ancestral lands, stewardship, and voices of the non-human. I began deconstructing my own patterns and hidden desires while breaking open ochres, clay, and dirt to make paints—a somatic practice of 'grounding with ground.' I ended up producing over forty small paintings, created a TVP color palette from the rock beach, attempted to begin a garden full of dye plants, experimented with cyanotypes, paper making, encaustic, and basket weaving, and I even produced some electronic music with the help of the creek and Shannon's husband, who has a wealth of knowledge. Every day felt unbelievably expansive.

TVP provided a container for me to grow, learn, and lean into inevitable cycles of change. I so appreciate my time with Shannon, her family, and her incredible art residency. This experience has been invaluable and connective, and I am so excited to one day return.

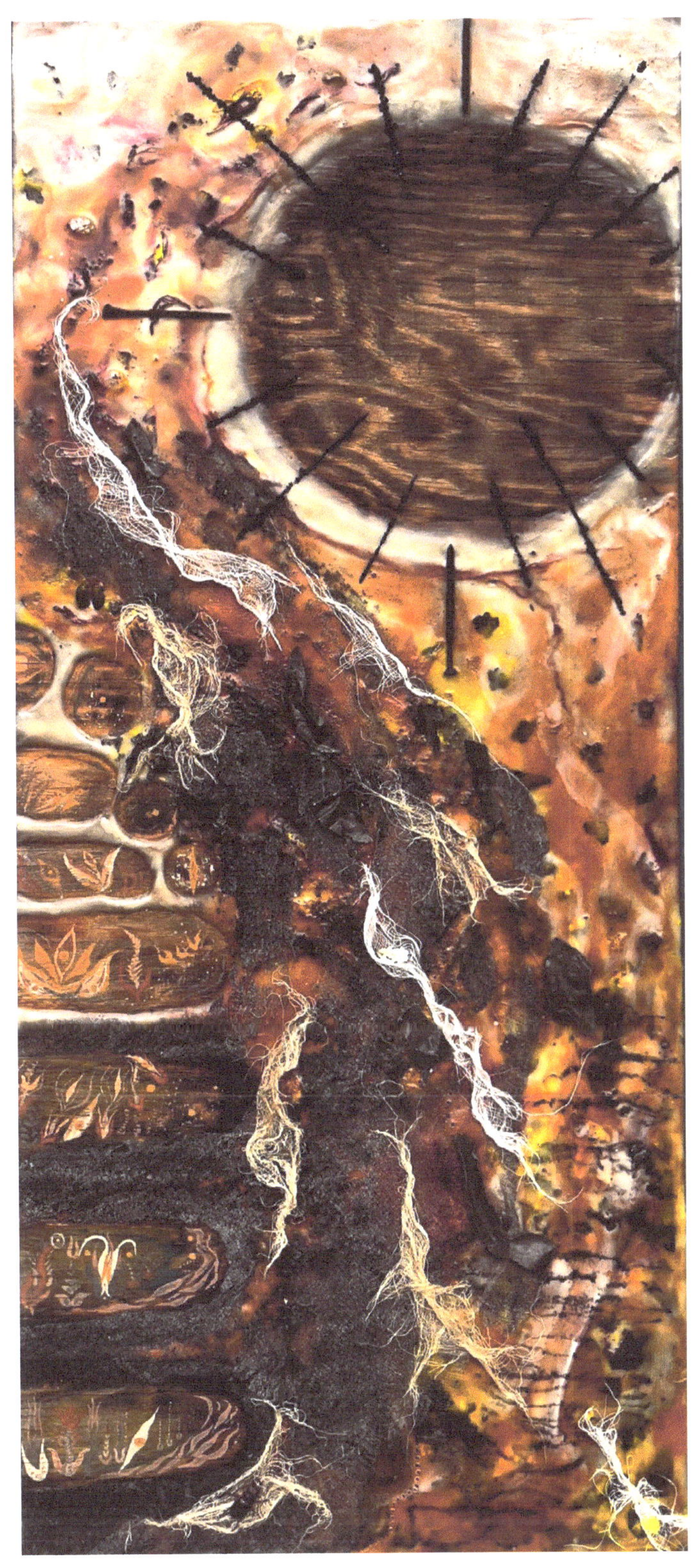

Kacy McKinney

For the duration of the residency, I am basically living outside, which is completely different from my experience of creating art in my own studio. As an avid birder, I usually go out birding and then come home to draw or paint. I don't do plein air work because when I am birding, I want to be completely absorbed in listening/witnessing/following my senses, and when I am drawing I want all of the comforts of a studio. With The Verdancy Project, I can have it all at once. Since I am cooking and bathing and working and birding and eating and sleeping either outside or at least much closer to it, it's as if there is no divide between the natural environment and the creative process. This absence of a boundary means that I am active in my creative process throughout the entirety of the residency, day and night and during every activity—it's very exciting and lends itself to experimentation. This drawing was completely different from anything I had created up to that point and it has everything to do with the influence of so much consistent time outside.

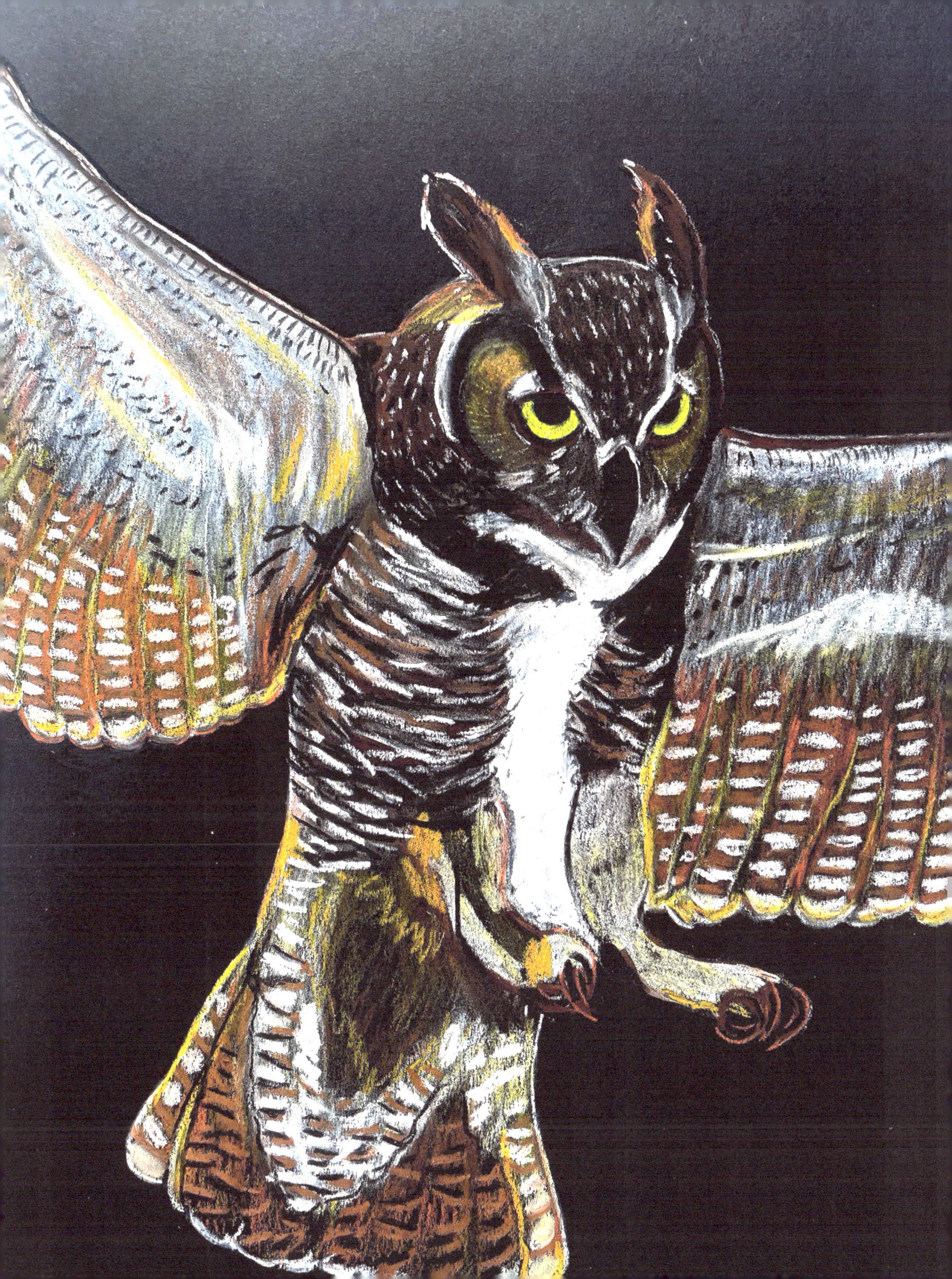

Bobb Amidon

A soundscape composed of found sounds from The Verdancy Project property (animals, creek, wind, banging on tree stumps, etc.) and synthetic sounds mimicking the natural sounds. The rhythmic cues come from the rhythm of birdsong, chicken calls, and woodpeckers. Using chance algorithms, the audio is ever-changing and will never be exactly the same twice.

Scan to listen

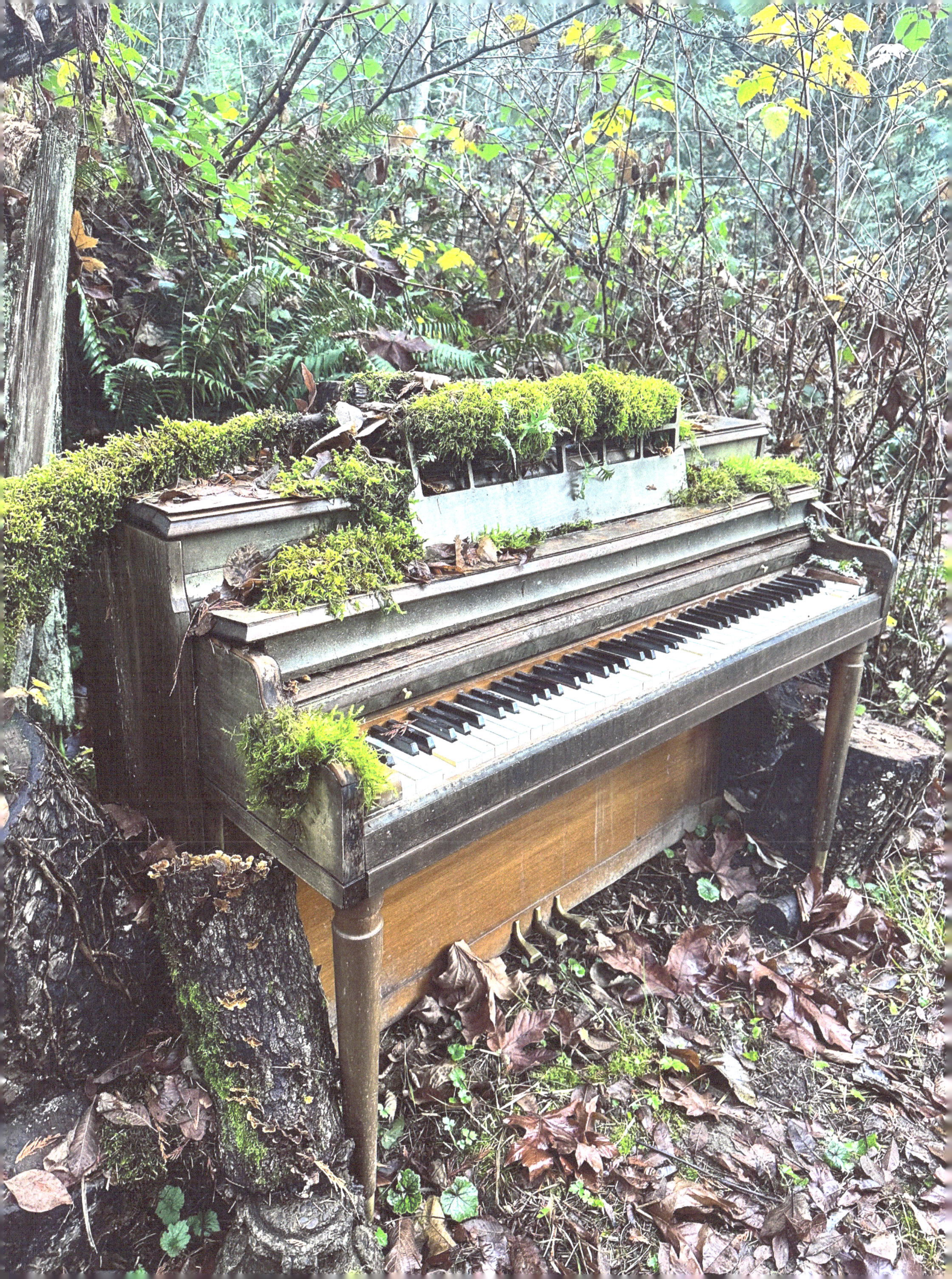

Contributing Artist Info

Amber Wolf
PO Box 15126, Portland, OR 97293

Amy Ash
www.amyash.ca

Anna Czoski
art.czoski.com

Anne Mavor
www.annemavor.com

Barb Burwell
www.barb-burwell.com

Bedrock Theatre
www.bedrocktheatre.com

Beth Wilson
BWilsonArt.com

Brittney Corrigan
brittneycorrigan.com

Bobb Amidon
soundcloud.com/bobb-amidon

Brooke Kuhnhausen
verdancyproject.com/brookekuhnhausen

Conor Eifler
conoreifler.com

Corey S. Pressman
coreypressman.com

Erica Gibson
ericagibson.com

Jim Stewart
zymoglyphic.org/about.html

Joellen Sweeney
joellensweeney.com

Juliet Johnson
julietjohnson.art

Kacy McKinney
www.kacymckinney.com/

Kendra Larson
www.kendralarson.com

Leiana Petlewski
www.instagram.com/leiana.petlewski

Linda Robertson
www.LindaRobertsonArts.com

Magda Permut
www.magdapermutphd.com

Merridawn Duckler
www.instagram.com/merridawnduckler

Morgan Barnett
www.morgancbarnett.com

ProLab Dance
prolabdance.com

Rose Covert
www.instagram.com/gatesofmystery

Sabin Timalsena
sabin.art

Sami Wax
samiwax.com

Sharon Servilio
www.sharonservilio.com

Shelly Smith
www.studiocornix.com

Sierra Weir
www.instagram.com/sierraweir

The Verdancy Project
www.verdancyproject.com

Gratitude & Acknowledgments

The Verdancy Project would not be what it is today without the generosity, support, and belief of so many people. This space is built not just on land, but on the dedication, kindness, and contributions of a community that has nurtured it into what it has become.

First and foremost, **Bobb and Sabine Amidon**, your unwavering support, encouragement, and belief in me and this project have been nothing short of extraordinary. Your generosity and love have made this all possible.

To our past and present board of advisors, **Christine Rasmussen**, **Joellen Sweeney**, **Brooke Kuhnhausen**, and **Amber Wolf.** Your thoughtful guidance, expertise, and encouragement have helped shape so many of our projects, events, and initiatives. Your insights continue to help us grow in ways we never could have imagined.

A special thanks to **Barb Burwell**, our very first resident, who bravely embraced the unknown and helped shape the artist residency aspect of The Verdancy Project. Your trust and enthusiasm set the foundation for everything that followed.

Deep gratitude to **Donny Foley** for donating our bookshed and to **Jim Stewart** for filling it with so many wonderful books. To **Alasdair Mackenzie**, whose incredible bee trees have brought life and movement to the land in ways we never expected.

To **Lacey Bryant, Elba Raquel, Sabine Amidon** and **Kacy McKinney**, for adorning our walls and surroundings with beautiful depictions of the birds and insects on the land. Your artwork is enjoyed and admired by all who visit.

Deepest thanks to **Rachel Warren** for your invaluable guidance and editorial support in shaping this anthology. Your insight, care, and expertise are deeply appreciated.

To our **instructors**, who have shared their wisdom, creativity, and passion through workshops and classes; your teaching has inspired countless moments of wonder.

To all the **artists, creatives, and dreamers** who have come through these doors; you are the beating heart of this space, and your presence, work, and ideas make it what it is.

And finally, to our **incredible community**, those who attend our events, workshops, and gatherings, who share their stories, who bring their curiosity, donate to the artists and who continue to support this vision—thank you. You remind us why this work matters, and we are endlessly grateful.

About the Editor

Shannon Amidon is the founder and director of The Verdancy Project, a multidisciplinary, community-rooted arts and ecology initiative based in the Pacific Northwest. Through this multi-faceted endeavour, which includes an artist-in-residence program, creative workshops, research initiatives, and community art projects, she cultivates spaces for curiosity, connection, and environmental stewardship.

An artist, beekeeper, environmental steward, and wonder seeker, Shannon has participated in artist residencies around the world, focusing on both art-making and ecological research. She has collaborated with scientists, artists, activists, and researchers across disciplines, and her work has been exhibited internationally in both solo and group exhibitions. Her creative efforts have been supported by numerous grants and awards, including the Regional Arts & Culture Council Make|Learn|Build Grant, International Encaustic Artists Project Grant, Silicon Valley Creates Artist Laureate, and others.

Residency highlights include The Ayatana Artistic Research Program (Canada), Herhusid House (Iceland), The David and Julia White Artist Colony (Costa Rica), and Sou'wester (Washington). Her work is held in corporate collections such as Google, Genentech, Wells Fargo, Imagery Estate Winery, and Kaiser Permanente.

You can find her at www.shannonamidon.com

Image Index

Page 4 - The Verdancy Project Treehouse

Page 7 - Shannon Amidon, Founder and Director of The Verdancy Project Photograph by Stephanie Honeycutt

Page 9 - Beaver Creek

Page 10 - **Top Left**: Buried Book Project. **Top Right:** Beaver Creek. **Bottom**: Bees, bats and butterflies painted on the main house by Lacey Bryant, and Elba Raquel

Page 11 - **Top Left:** Tree stump fairy circle. **Top Right**: Beaver Creek. **Bottom Left**: Beaver Creek. **Bottom Right**: TVP Chipmunk

Page 12 - Canvas bell tent, the very first sleeping accomodations

Page 13 - Current sleeping caravan

Page 14 - **Top**: Snowy field - TVP in Winter. **Bottom:** Snow-covered Beaver Creek

Page 15 - **Top Left**: Dye garden. **Top Right**: Tea towels dyed with plants from dye garden. **Bottom**: Beaver Creek with gazing bench

Page 16 - **Left**: Bookshed with bird paintings by Kacy McKinney. **Top Right**: Book shed interior. **Bottom Right**: Books in book shed

Page 17 - **Top Left**: Bee tree log hive courtesy of Alasdair Mackenzie. **Bottom Left**: A few of the TVP hens. **Right**: Beaver Creek woods

Page 18 - Beaver Creek

Page 19 - The Verdancy Project field and creek in autumn

Page 20 - Students in journaling workshop

Page 21 - **Top Left**: Students taking natural pigment workshop. **Top Right**: Students in Lumen Printing workshop. **Bottom**: Students in paper flower workshop

Page 22 - Art and Seed Swap seed packets laid out

Page 23 - **Top**: 2021 seed-packet art. **Bottom**: 2025 seed-packet art

Page 24 - **Left**: Madeline Ross singing opera in Beaver Creek. **Left:** Maria Olaya serenading guest at our Spring Seed Session

Page 25 - **Left**: Lisa Gilham, Jenny Bunce, and Jessica Zodrow performing a Mary Oliver poem at our Autumn Seed Session. **Right**: Briana Ratterman Trevithic singing and storytelling at our Winter Seed Session

Page 26 - **Top**: Conor Eifler sharing an original short story at our Summer Seed Session. **Bottom**: Summer altar created by Brooke Kuhnhausen

Page 27 - **Top**: Alasdair Mackenzie talking about natural beekeeping at our Summer Seed Session. **Bottom**: Shannon Amidon talking with guests, Photograph by Brooke Kuhnhausen

Page 28 - **Left:** *Beacon Creek* Sculpture, Corey Pressman, Photograph by Stephanie Honeycutt. **Right**: *North Fork Beaver Creek Waterlines | 45°29'48.1"N 122°21'00.7"W* by Clairissa Stephens, Photograph by Stephanie Honeycutt

Page 29 - **Top**: *The Night the Stars Fell,* Jocelyn Rice. **Bottom**: *The Night the Stars Fell interior* by Jocelyn Rice, Photographs by Stephanie Honeycutt

Page 30 - **Top**: *Metamorphic Lessons from Nature: Decomposition, Transmutation and Reformation,* Amanda Triplett, Photograph by Stephanie Honeycutt. **Bottom**: *Bird Watching,* choreographer Ruth Nelson, Owl dancer Amelia Logan, Photograph by Stephanie Honeycutt

Page 31 - **Top**: *Large Obsidian Windchime*, Deborah & Richard Bloom, Photograph by Stephanie Honeycutt. **Bottom**: *Chrysalis Pods* by Francisca Lauren Carrera, Bee tree installation by Alasdair Mackenzie Photograph by Stephanie Honeycutt

Page 33 - You are magic card by Amulette Studios, Photograph by Brooke Kuhnhausen

Page 35 - *Altars of Belonging,* Strawflowers, moss, tree bark, Brooke Kuhnhausen, Photograph by Stephanie Honeycutt

Page 37 - Joellen Sweeney as Bog Woman

Page 39 - *Stream Guardian,* fabric, Papier-mâché , wax, paint, Joellen Sweeney

Page 41 - Brittney Corrigan reading from her book *Daughters* at the Autumn Seed Session

Page 42- Moon over The Verdancy Project

Page 45 - **Top left**: Sunflowers, ink, and art-making materials. **Top Right**: In process painting. **Bottom**: *Nature Laughed in the Sun,* Acrylic on pearlescent canvas, 24" x 36", Linda Robertson, created with plants, flowers, sticks and stream water sourced from The Verdancy Project

Page 47 - **Top:** *Woven Willow Den,* Willow, Rose Covert. **Bottom**: Entrance to *Woven Willow Den* with Rose Covert inside, Photographs by Stephanie Honeycutt

Page 48 - *Constellation,* Willow, 14" x 14" x 4", Rose Covert

Page 49 - *Consonance,* Willow, 14" x 14" x 4", Rose Covert

Page 51 - Animated projection-mapped installation on Rose Covert's willow, Anna Czoski and Sabin Timalsena

Page 55 - *Wise Cedar,* Earth pigments, tree, Erica Gibson

Page 59 - *The Mossarium: A Cryptobiotic Ecosystem,* moss, rocks, bark, fish tank, Jim Stewart

Page 61 - **Top**: *A catalogue of gifts to red cedar,* rocks, thread, Juliet Johnson.
Bottom: *A catalogue of gifts to red cedar (detail),* rocks, thread, Juliet Johnson

Page 65 - *Unfurling,* Leiana Petlewski and Jaren Kerr, Photographs by Jaren Kerr

Page 67 - **Left**: Stoneware epiphyte vessel, 3" x 7", Morgan Barnett.
Right: Hagstone and thorn bowl set, 8"x 8" and 4" x 4", Morgan Barnett

Page 69 - *Microbial Forms,* Watercolor on paper, Shelly Smith

Page 71 - Spiral Shell, Photograph, Magda Permut

Page 75 - *The Sex Life of Flowers*, stoneware with glaze and underglaze, hemp twine, wood beads, metal clasps, dimensions variable, approx 8" x 20" x 16", Sharon Servilio

Page 77 - **Top**: *Cycles of Sustenance*, multi-exposure cyanotype on cotton, mounted on wood, 60" x 57", Amy Ash, Photograph by Naomi Peters. **Bottom**: *Embracing Rest (to bloom again)*, cyanotype, beeswax, dye, mounted on wood, 10" tondo, Amy Ash, Photograph by Caleb Jones

Page 79 - **Top**: *The Nature Bar*, Bedrock Theatre, left to right, Joellen Sweeney, Sean Grosshans, Richard Bloom. **Bottom**: Bedrock Theatre, left to right, Emily Eisele, Joellen Sweeney, Sean Grosshans, Photographs by Stephanie Honeycutt

Page 81 - *High Desert Phases*, Acrylic on canvas, 40" x 60", Kendra Larson

Page 83 - **Top**: *Place No. 1*, Mixed fiber, 6" x 6" x 1.5". **Bottom**: *Clothwork 3*, Mixed fiber, 10" x 10 "x 1.5", Barb Burwell

Page 85 - *Between*, Laura Cannon - dancer, Lynne Piper - vocalist , Sculpture by Andy Kennedy, Photographs by Stephanie Honeycutt

Page 87 - **Left**: *Secret Path*, botanical contact prints on vintage hemp canvas and reused linen, locally harvested bamboo. Plants: bracken fern, vitex, geranium, rose, marigold, mulberry, 38" x 16", Anne Mavor. **Right**: *Black Walnut Being*, botanical contact print with black walnut, ginkgo, and marigold on reused linen, locally harvested bamboo, 47" x 26", Anne Mavor, Photographs by Aaron Wessling

Page 88 - *Trio: Seeking Synergy*, Reclaimed agriculture tarp, synthetic twine, acrylic paint, mirrors, 20' x 20' x 1', Beth Wilson

Page 89 - *Nest of Nettles: Sitting with my Pioneer Ancestry*, Wild harvested stinging nettles, antique lace and ribbon, sticks, approx 5' wide x 2.5' tall, Photograph by Stephanie Honeycut

Page 91 - Amber Wolf examining her buried book

Page 93 - *the woods know what to do with a body*, Video still, Sami Wax

The Verdancy Project is a multidisciplinary, community-centered initiative dedicated to fostering curiosity and inspiring environmental stewardship. We offer creative residencies, retreats, community art projects, events, and workshops. We provide a unique opportunity to reflect, create, and explore in an inspiring setting in the Pacific Northwest.

We believe in the creative relationship between the land, art, and science.

Verdancy / VUR-duhn-see / *Noun*: The lush appearance of flourishing vegetation. Greenness, verdure. Type of: cornucopia, profuseness, profusion, richness. The property of being extremely abundant.

www.ingramcontent.com/pod-product-compliance
Ingram Content Group UK Ltd.
Pitfield, Milton Keynes, MK11 3LW, UK
UKHW060117300726
14090UKWH00002B/245
* 9 7 9 8 9 9 9 3 8 6 4 0 3 *